AMERICAN EQUATIONS IN BLACK CLASSICAL MUSIC

Counting the Beat: Blues Time and Temporal Alchemy

POEMS
Camae Ayewa

HAT & BEARD PRESS | LOS ANGELES

Dedicated to my Family

My Grandmother & Great Grandmother & Great Great Grandmother's name is Ella so you can call me Lady Time

Muddy Waters. 2017. Courtesy Alison Saar.

CONTENTS

Torch Song. 2019. Courtesy Alison Saar.

Jazz O.P.U.S.

Generational Griots & African Temporal Orchestration

Jazz Opus the Odes 100192 Generational Griots
Origins of Power Unspoken Scores In Black 9
Classical Music Divertimento 1 jazz root 1 01 198 22
I used this title Jazz not as definition of a style 9 8
of music but merely as an agent of memory 100110
Jazz In The Red/BLACK root 0 1 jazz root 100
Mapping Inequalities in the Red jazz root 0978765
 jazz 00 11 root 01010 jazz 09 Black Classical Cadence
Musical Poetry of African root systems jazz root jazz
root 101100 jazz 0011 root 01 0 10 Jasm 97800090
INDUSTRIES zz root root 01 jazz 0 jazz 11 root 10 jazz
root root 011 Compendium of Poetry and Music root 10
jazz root 0 jazz 11 root 10 jazz root root 011892930400
Jasm *INDUSTRIES AT THE McComas Institute 90*

Haiku 'Round Moonlight For Hazel Scott

Blues Show 'Round Midnight Trinidad Caribbean Sound of a New World

Black Woman

I Found Myself Listening To Linda Sharock
I Found Myself Praying Thank You
Black Woman
Voice Healing
I Searched For You
Your Voice Vibration Cured
Curved Space
Dreaming Galactic Formations
A Message From The Nile
Like A River We Listen
Black Woman Confessions

Diamond Teeth Mary
Bessie Smith
Memphis Minnie
We Hear You
15th Ward Moans
Willie Mae Thornton
Ma Rainey
We Listen Our Hearts Hungry
Vi Redd
Clora Bryant
Shirley Scott
BLUES SERENADERS
Survival Blues
Soon And Very Soon
Kula-Mae
Victory Will Be Ours

I've Got A Home On Dat Rock It Won't Be Long
Hold On
Hold On Sisters
We Hear You Moaning
We Don't Need No Words
We Made Our Own Language
Black Woman Blues Technology

Watching The StarShips Come In

An ARKESTRA
A Sun Ra Myth Arkestra
A Sonic Dance
In The Garden Of Far Out Truths & Lived Experience
Just Ask Marshall Allen
99 YEARS
Never Seen Hands Like His Before
Hands That Stretch Out Into The Future

Sun Ra Said Don't Need No Grave No Headstone / No Casket
       I Am Not Only Here I Am Constantly Returning
                (Was Not Never But Always)
Secrets Of The Sun Interstellar Loways
Sun Ra Said These Artists Are Thieves
Just Angels And Demons At Play

In Search Of Other Voices
In Search Of Other Blues
In Search Of Our Mothers Starships
In Search of STAR Reflections
Blues De - Lights De - Gospel Train
Sounds Of Joy Astro Black in Feeling
This is what it feels like to hear us
Feels like making dreams come true
Outer Spaceways /Quantum Ways of Inner Science /*Black Rainbow Myths*
Far Out In Space Sound Mirrors
Mirror Time Mirror Time Mirror
BLACK QUANTUM Astro Infinities
Let The Shadows Take Shape and guide us into the
Shadow Museum
Just Before The Music
JUST BEFORE EARTH

Spaceship Lullabies
I am Apart Of The Wonder
Lonnie's Hands Like Marshall's
THE AGE OF A WAVE DRAWING THE ART OF LIFE
Water Spooks & Spirits Staying Alive Breathing Blues

These are the stories of our Ancestors. Thoughts like light trapped in Prisms

Ancient To The Future

Sirius Calling
An Art Ensemble In The Future Make A Stop In Paris
An Advancement In Creative Music

The Meeting
50 Years In The Body Of Sound
Ancient To The Future
Congo Ritual Of Fire
A Message To Our Folks
This Is A Love Thang
Sun Music Dancing With Our Fathers

Roscoe Mitchell Rap Fire 9 Am In The Morning Full Suit On
Talking About
50 Years Ancient To The Past
Joseph Jarman The Poets Poet
Wood Stained Words Loud Ears Hearts Feedback
A Fundamental Destiny
A Love Message Ancient Before Feeling
Art Ensemble Of Soweto
We Prayed for you
Thunder Drums and Marimba Rain

Famoudou Don Moye Addressing The Elephant In The Room
Moor Music Moor Money Moor Mother Moor Freedom

Ohnedaruth!

A Organism
Naked
A Proximity To Life
We Got To Survive
Full Force Sound Heart
Blues And Mind

Pathways To Unknown Worlds
Intergalactic Research Nonaah Voyager
Liberation Sound
Once You Go Black You Can't Be In The RED

Spatial Aspects of The Sound
Moye Tutankhamun Sound Heart
Lester Bowie The Alternate Express
Roscoe Mitchell Heart Blues Mind Sunrise in Different Dimensions
When Angels Speak of Love
Muhal Richard Abrams
Fontella Bass
Martha Bass
From Paris to Chicago
An Ensemble of Seasons
Joseph Jarman Urban Magic
Malachi Favors, Wind and SUN Music
It's the Sign of the Times
A Theme
ODWALLA

THELONIOUS TIME

Monk's Mood
Monk's Dream
Monk's Muse
Monk's Blues
Monk's Mircules

Always on MONK'S Time

Miles and Monk Legacies
Monk and Trane Futures
Conversations with Thelonious Sphere Monk
Straight no chaser closer to the truth

Mighty Blue Monk
Bolivar Monk
San Juan Hill Monk
Monk Rhythm -a-ning
Monk Gonna Rock, Around the Clock Tonight
Break the Clock Tonight
Smash the master's Clock Tonight

11 - *Six Six Six After Death Notes*

Blue Note Boys Gon Get Ya
What Ya Gon Do
A Belly Empty Impulse
Can't Be No Rat
If You Don't Sign That Universal Contract
Yo Cabaret Card Gon Get Suspended
IRS Gon Come Take Yo Voice
Take Yo Space
Leave No Oxygen

Send You Back In Time
Send You Back To The Junk Joint
Fatback Chitlin Circuit
Back To Community Economics (Not A Bad Idea)

Nights Like This I Wish The Sky Would Just Fall

The Newport Rebels

We still hear you as we stomp out newports on new york streets
fuck yo festival fuck yo jazz
you ain't got what we got
we got time machines
don't make us take a trip down memory lane
come back air things out

political sonics

II
when the clock frieze/froze

                    art so cold

white walls of melting ice

                  flood coming

Little Richard's Revenge
Fire and blues on the USS Independence

The vaults of RCA Victor
Peacock Records
Specialty Records
Sputnik 1
Broken
Dated
Satellites
Crashing Down
Bits and pieces of a life

GateMouth Brown African Fiddle Playing By and By
Dianne Reeves and Anita Baker Singing on the Restless Sea of Time

Dolphy Blues

Out in the world
Just you and your horn
Playing far out and free with all kinds of cats
People gon start thinking u crazy
Gon think you hooked on drugs
Playing as out as you do
The anti of everything linear
Hard Bop Inventions

And that was the case
Being misunderstood
No matter what stage
What club
What festival
Doing this jazz thing & breaking every rule they hold dear

(the gag is they not even music people, we have no record of them, actually feeling)

Don't Make Me Call Art Blakey, Tony Williams, Elvin Jones, Tony Allen

Tell Them To Bring The Drum
The Jungle
The Protest
The Sugar Cane Molasses
The Rhythm
The Spirit
The Swinging Machete From Barbados

Shut This Thing Down Real Quick

Just Ask The BLUES

BESSIE SMITH said I'm Not BLUE
I'm BLACK, RED, GOLD, PURPLE, INDIGO
I'm Not 1930
I'm 1884 1920 2033 1970 1949 1994
Ask MAHALIA JACKSON
See we serve the people
It was the people
Who helped me
When I was hungry
It was God
that held me in song
When I thought I had nothing left
Just like UNA MAE CARLISLE
They don't know me
Sweet hollering blues
Big Mama Thornton at the mic
Lord of Yellow Nu
Queen of the Valley
Lower South White Lily
Jamaican Black Rose
Myth Restoration
Sonic Juke
Mary Lou Williams Legend Has It You Birthed A Galaxy
Nina Simone Singing & Asking us are we ready
Really ready
To love
To listen
To be
African Women
Are you ready
Are you really ready
To speak
To dream
To cultivate
O/ur Power
O/ur Peace
O/ur Future

From The Desk of Davis & Coleman

The Problem With The Jazz Here
Is That They (The Audience)
Sleep Standing Up
Spilling Beer On Themselves
In The Cool Jazz On A Hot Summer Day

The Problem with the Jazz Here is the Money
Overdue
Overrun
and looking the other way

So you gotta respect the process of nothing
and walk out the room if it ain't swinging
walk out the room if it ain't saying something
If it ain't creating a possible future right in front of you
If it ain't got no meat, no bone, no marrow

The future
Already here
Smoke lust mirrors
See it don't mean a thing if it ain't got the blues
The forgotten voices of the blues
Evicted voices
Up out of the world voices
Inside of the earth voices
Down the street from Clarksville voices

Speak up because
Soon it will be a museum exhibit
A viral dance
A racist passing of time

Another Brick In The Wall
Another Building Ready To Be Sold
A Buying
A Selling
A Drunkness

Owner and Developer speaking (lying) to blurred residents (you & me)

Who still breathing on beat,
on cue, under the flashlight of demon-crazy?
I mean democracy
Who is still holding their breath?
Watching the clock
Watching the news
Waiting for the kids to come home at night
Watching and Waiting
Who is still in memory?
We shadows of uncertain truths must ask these questions

What has happened to us?
Jazz circuits
Sex fiends
Rock hazards
Thieves and knives
What has happened to us?
Money hounds
Monsters in the making
Bankrupted humanity
Guns and Ghosts
Death and Hollywood
Lies of Democracy
Spectators of Wars
What has happened to us?
Coded histories
Jasm witch trials
Slave Labor Camp Weddings
Cowboys and Girls
Running around the mountain Till he comes
Big Dick
Southern Cock
Church and State

Landlord and Developer

To bring us another war
Another empire
Another industry
Another poison
Another disease
Another nightmare

A Blues For Milford Graves

Part 1 *The Heart*

it's nature man
i wasn't playing around
see i went right to the source
i was reading all these books
about the masters going back to the source
you know up in the mountains
deep in meditation
it's nature man
i wasn't playing around
see i went right to the source
i went right to the heart
straight to the heart man

off beat off rhythm off time
this is what we sound like

ting-raww—frapt!
rat-a-tat-a-rot-a-toko!
shhhap
thwap!

off beat off rhythm off time
it's a different vibe man
we connected to a higher force
cosmic force call it whatever you want man
you know when your heart go
ting-raww—frapt!
rat-a-tat-a-rot-a-toko!
shhhap
thwap!

Part 2 *The Family*

This is a family
I wanna know how you doing today
I wanna know how you react to the rhythm
What is your heart saying
How fast you moving
How high is your highs
How low is yours blues
Listen to my heart
See this is swinging
Swinging in to the next day
Fist blazing
Drums blazing
Life moving on
A people move on
The rhythm moving on
A power

This is a family
We have our own teachers and only our hearts know their names
Ritual of secrecy
Can't give it all away
Especially when they can't hear it
When they can't taste it, can't feel it
When they can't smell it, can't see it
Listen to your heart
Feel it swinging
Swinging in to the next day
Blood blazing
Drums blazing
Life moving on
A people moving on
The rhythm moving on
A ritual surviving

Part 3 *Survival*

aye ay ay aye
visions visions
aye ay aye aye
visions of a liberated future

Took me to see Trane man
Those drums was loose
Free swinging
And I said I want to survive man
I want to survive
Like that
Martial arts
Freedom swinging
Survival
Come at me with everything you got
I wanna know what I need to work out
Survival
Eubie Blake
James P. Johnson
Scott Joplin
The King of Ragtime
A Communal Sound
Juba & Jubilee
Jelly Roll Morton
William Grant Still
Hall Johnson
John Wesley Work Sr
Will Marion Cook
The Origin of the Cakewalk

My friend went to Harvard man, only for a year man,
and came back home to teach the people everything he learned
See man, that's survival
Going back in the garden having a conversation
Listening to the rhythm around you
Juba Yara
Juba Yara
Survival

Part 4 *The Drum*

Cosmic energy
Dialogue of the drums
The vibration of the earth is changing
We need far out inner sounds
Sounds that are tuned in
Are you tuned in to
No time no time no time
No time no time no time
Just the drum
The heart
The drum
The heart

Aye man am I floating or flying?
Are you listening to the plants?
Are you sitting in the garden?

Space time, back in no time, beyond quantum's holy ghosts, pieces of time

Quantum Visions with Ra's Sun (jazz was gravity)

I am the uncollapse
information escaping
the continuation
A better understanding of gravity

I am the uncollapse
already on my way
light residue
scattered spirits

I am the unbothered
curved time
A known particle

Night Dreamers
Paean

Pick Up The Phone Man
It's Time To Get Going
You Ready Herbie?
Wayne, Bring That Notebook You Been Scribbling In
We Got Places To Go Far Out Imagine In ESP
Juju Beyond Infinity
Night Dreamers in Love
The All Seeing Eye Knows all cosmic connections
Did you know Sunlight Secrets hold possibilities
We Got Inventions And Dimensions
We Dark Magus Star People Light Hours Ahead Of Time

Art Blakey & Cecil Taylor Jazz Messengers from Nubia Space
Abdullah Ibn Buhaina
Year 1919 Radio Raheem Blasting Rammellzee
Drums In The Rain
Hard Bop Thunder
Luminous Clouds Rosetta's Rain
Seventeen Messengers Bringing New Sounds
Fletcher Henderson, Reggie Workman at Birdland
Lee Morgan, Freddie Hubbard, Benny Golson, Sarah Vaughan
Kenny Dorham, Hank Mobley in the Field Calls To Prayer
You can hear Milton Nascimento, McCoy Tyner and Donald Byrd
coming
Drums Around The Corner
BLUES MARCH TIME MACHINE
Cecil Taylor Unit Structures
Feel The Air above the Mountains
Feel The Air
Can you feel the Love
The Love for Sale
The Love below our Feet
AMEWA

Betty Carter For President

Betty Bebop The Modern Sound
Round Midnight & It Ain't About The Melody!

Le Magic Scat
Scatting The Blues
Scat Us A Genius
Scat Us Out Of Darkness
Melancholy Momentum Space Garden

Black Women
Scat Us A Dream
Scat Us Into A New Century

A good tone is rare, it attacks the heart new rhythms, halos and inventions

you
me
our
home
our
body
our
Breath

In harmony

This Blues Here Is For Dizzy

Good Night Jazz Fire
Smoke Desire Praise
Drum Drunk Crash
Hands Burnt Coal
New Comings
Dripping Dizzy
Wet Coltrane
Dee Dee Bridgewater
Blue Miles

We Ready
The Boats Coming In
We Bridges Of Many Backs
We Communal Winds Of Change
We Ready

Hey Man, Look Here, You See These 88 Keys?

Black & White Unity

Ok Now Look Again
See It Aint No Unity
No Black
No White
No Together
No Nothing

Just The Blues

One Color
A Blues Ideology

JUST A FEW OF *My favorite things*
In the future, waking up, heart streaming what's left of the material world

      Someone, PLEASE PLEASE Sound The Trumpet's

Triumph

All For Buddy Bolden
The Color Of New Orleans Zero Before Earth Afrofuturism

Cornet King Bolden Baptist Church
Buddy Bolden Blues
Mound Bayou Mississippi
Bunk Johnson
Funky Butt Philosophies
Cape Fear River Highway
Hambone Physics
Doreen Ketchens
The Sounds of East Louisiana
Dippermouth Blues
Doctor Jazz
Bill Robinson
Jackson Ward
Cab Calloway's Jitterbug party
Ascension Parish
Lincoln Gardens
Sunset Cafe
Buck and Wing Tabernacle
Hotcha Razz-Ma-Tazz
Creole Jazz Band banned from Congo Square
Canal Street Blues
Sugar Foot Stomp
The Great Depression
Hard Times I Sold my Trumpet in Savannah

II
Here Comes Jazz Man Zero !
From Outer Space New Orleans
Here To Bring Us The Blues
The Rag Time
Le Jazz Man Zero
Our Hero Le Jazz Man Zero
Le Jazz Man Zero
Father Of Free Sound Swinging
Le Jazz Man Zero
Here To Save The Day
To Save The Sound

Dancing Mind

First Bass Line Loop We Had Was Mingus Ah Um

Didn't Know It Would Power My
Life Voice Activation
Life Art Aviation
Life Force Action
Didn't Know I Would Take Flight !

See Music Is The Tide
The Coming Home
The Returning
See Music Is The No Beat
The No Time
The Off & Future
The Far Out & Gone
Space Odyssey
The Circle And Her Spiral
Blues Roots & Jazz Experiments
Mysterious Blues

Meet Me Tonight At Noon I'll show you what's possible
I want something more for me
Something more for alla us
Especially those of us
Deep in Dope
Deep in Depression
Deep in Disappointment
Deep in Doubt
Deep in Decline
Deep in the Dense Daze

In Each Life Some Rain Must Fall
Ella Flying Home At The Savoy

Hello Again 1919
From The Depths Of Everything I Know

I Seent It
The Color Of Sound

And The Hell/Heaven It Came From

Stormy Weather
Plantation Revenue
Black Bottom
Mamba's Daughters

In A Nightclub On Juniper Street
I Was Never A Child
I Was Born Warrior Crowned Queen!

And They Tried It !

They Tried To Book Ella!

Ella
Went To Jail
Fur
Makeup
Crowned
Queen
Of
Time

A hundred years from now
Don't blame me
Don't worry about me
I got rhythm
I'm thriving on a riff

Lil Hardin Armstrong & Mae Barnes

One Thing About Swing
About New Orleans
About The Blues
About Jazz
About This Life

It's Ours And Ours Alone & Don't Nobody Own The Melody

Not On My Mind.
Not On My Mind
What People Think
They Not Known Of Dey Own Selves
Blues And Memory Free And Lost

Not On My Mind What They Think
Not On My Mind What They Think Of Me
They Not Known Of Dey Own Selves
Blues and memory free and lost

Not On My Mind
We Swinging
Soul to Soul
Back To Black
A FUTURE REAL
A P-FUNK BOOM BAP BEBOP
A HENDRIX DUET WITH OUR MEMORIES
A Blues Reel/Relic/Reality
Reel Life Entities/Identities/Ideologies

> *See it was never about jazz*
> *Fuck jazz*
> *This is creative music*
> *This ain't no Jam or no School Band*
> *This Is Real Life Futures*
> *Space Boat Histories*

The Fire Of Sound For The Love Of You
Le Codes Supreme - AN OPERA SHORT- mezzo soprano

The Sweat Of A Dream
Hanging Over Me
Singing Sweet Blues
Sweet Indigos
Summer Breeze
All The While In This Terror
You Can't Hold No Dream Captive
You Can't Beat Imagination Out Of The Mind
As Long As You Got A Heart Beating
You Got Music
And Don't Nobody
Own The Melody

A Love Supreme
A Love Supremus
Liebe Superus
Hearts Ome
Liubi Ohm Ohm Hymn
Lufu O Mh Hertz
Ome Hearts Ohm
Home Om Ohms
Between Heaven And Earth
Ascendere

Supreme Love
Supreme Being
I'm Coming Back Weeping Willows Swaying Ghosts

Fly Charlie Fly

Bird Set Loose In Our Dreams
Bird Set Loose In The Moonlight
In The Blue Light
The Night Light
The Black Light

Into The Shadow
This Is Classical Art
African Architecture
New Ark Screams Into The Unknown

Bird Set Loose In Our Dreams
Bird Set Loose In The Moonlight
In The Blue Light
The Night Light
The Black Light

Now We See The
Lady In The Moonlight
Lady In The Blue Light
Lady In The Night Light
Lady In The Black Light
Lady In The Shadow
Now We See Ourselves Enchanted

It's Time For New Visions
Feel The Vibrational Blues Of The Earth
Ghetto Lights Of Morning Prayers
We Need Complete Communion Spiritual Dialogue
Meet Me Back at the Chicken Shack
Bebop Blue Light Til Dawn Mount Parnassus
Searching For a New Landscape

Genius + Soul = A Jazz memory
See We Got All the Magic
African American Classical Music
A Jewel in the Lotus
Alchemy all up in the music
Divination
Inner Sight

One for Archie

Momma these contracts too tight
Rent too high
Sometimes I feel like a nationless child
This Blues a prayer
A song for Africa
A song for Malcolm
A song for our Mother
A song for our Future
Our future is a ballad for our children
Let them rest in melodies of peace
Come Sunday
We may all be singing Attica Blues
Come Sunday
We may all be singing nobody knows the trouble I've seen
Fire is/was the way ahead
On this night we goin home
On this night we going home
We crossing ocean bridges
Coral rocks
With a rose for Mama
On this night we going home
Down home
Splashes of memory
Life consequences
Ballads for trane
I hear the sound
I hear the sound
One for Archie
I hear the sound
Gold and silver
Fire and brimstone
See there's a trumpet in my soul
I can't shake the melody
I can't shake the poetry
It won't let me go

Black Quilts & Black Maps Quilting Codes

It is a Jazz Math Language situation
It is a Ritual
just watch ***Muhal Richard Abrams on stage***
It is a Myth Science
Anthropology of Consciousness Language
Ocean Biology
Sonic Horticulture
It's like sitting in the Garden with ***Anthony Braxton***

Physics Sacred Geometry

Go Listen to Anthony Braxton. Tell me what do you see?

the circulus
circling in
circle in the round
the inner circle
enter space exit time
concentric circles
protection
the magic circle
circle waltz
(sabar)

Heaven Within The Cosmos
Godhead
Halo
Radii
Annulus
Mandala
The Turning Wheel
Moon Time

Photographs

Ma Rainey
She Just Like Me
No Pictures Of Me Growing
A Future
A Freedom
Sonic Portals

New York To Memphis
Late Night Sweat Cloud
Foundations Crumbles
Futures Iron Out

All That History
Dust And Stars
African Skin On Wood

Ma Rainey
Moaning In
Moaning Out
Ask Me What I Sing And I'll Tell You
It's The Blues
Assassination Blues
Black Frequencies
Language Of What It Means
The Blues
Dark Brown Lovers Swim
Big Feeling Blues
None Of Your Bizness Blues
I'm In Love Moonshine Blues
Blues The World Forgot
The Blues Remembers Everything The Country Forgot
Blues Oh Blues
Bleeding Heart Blues
Seeking Blues
Woman To Woman Night Time Blues
Dream Blues
I'm Gonna Sing Til The Spirit Moves Blues

I know I can Love You Better

How do Max Roach & Abbie Lincoln hold up the pyramids from Newport to East Harlem?

It's A Landscape Full Of Color
Black Mountains & Blue Birds
You Know
Like Woody Shaw Live At The Village Vanguard
Lady Noon
Sun Light Sweet Music
We Hear Them
Vultures Circling
We Not Afraid
Ask Dinah Washington
Ask Nicole Mitchell

We Not Afraid
We Got The Healing Force
Universal Force *Of Pharaoh Sanders*
We Got The Healing Force
The Universal Force *Of Alice Coltrane*
Let Us Join Hands And Chant

note
We need to learn how to protect each other
How to move through depression
How to deal with the world when you tell your truth
When you defend the Rights of African people
See It Aint Easy
The weight of the world will crush you
Leave you just ass and asphalt
No bootstrap to pick you up just a boot to knock you down
See cats ain't really talking about it they rather leave legacies in tact
But life is life man
We break it apart and put it back together
Being a woman, in Jazz, in Blues, in Hip Hop, in America, in Europe, shit the whole world -These men think they created us

The Birth of Cool
Let Us Preserve These Histories For Duke & Everybody Else

The Duke Of Mississippi
Duke Ellington
Holy Water Rag
Sir Jelly Roll Morton & His Vast Kingdoms Of God And Gold

See I Was On The Corner Real Life Sounds
Ask *Miles*

I Heard It All
Joe Mcphee
Said It's Nation Time For Real This Time
The Do Over, The Time Machine, The Portal

The Future Is Now
It's Time We Get Some Understanding
Roy Brooks With Woody Shaw & Carlos Garnett

Black Dada
Alberta Hunter
Memphis Downhearted Blues
Horace Silver Wipe Away the Evil
The Book Of Monk Funk Lore

It's Time We Get Some Understanding
One In Two Out The Rat Race
Two In One Out The Death Race
Max And Dizzy Out of the Past
Bright Moments In Bright Mansions Once Again
In The Light Holy Ghosts We /Remember Clifford Brown
Jazz Contrast in the Multiverse
Newport Rebels Yell Redemption
Tain't Nobody's Bizness If I Do
Ask Abbie Lincoln
In the Red Retribution
The Big Payback and I want it all
I want it all back everything I deserve

Lady Day / April 7th

I Wanna Smoke A Cig With Billie
And Change What Happened / What Keeps Happening
To All Us Singing Blues Gals

On The Cotton - Chitterling -Internet - Euro - Internet Circuits

Sing The Song
Lady Day Sing The Song
Let Them Know
Sing The Song
And Let Them Know
Smooth Sailing On Your Last Breath Out Of Here
It Was Beautiful
And It Wasn't The Drugs
It Was Never The Drugs
What They Can Do To You Is Stronger Than Any Drug
It's The Weight Of The Southern Breeze
It's The Baritone Of Sweets Lows And Sweet Chariots Coming To Take
Us Home
Casting Us Out The Theater Of Freedom
The Pretending To Be All Right In Our Solitude
Taunted By Memories That Never Die

Ode To Mary

My Momma
Pinned A Rose On Me
I Went To See
Mary Lou Williams

Mary Played Scorpio
Ran Them Keys Back Inside The Piano
Free Spirits
Free Truth
Free In The Air
So Sharp
B Sharp
C Sharp
So Sharp They Bleed
My Momma
Pinned A Rose On Me
My Momma Pinned The Rosary
I Went To See Mary Lou Williams

Mary Lou Williams Her Own Worlds

I Saw
People In Trouble
Praise The Lord

The Blues
Free Spirits
It Ain't Necessarily So
Praise The Lord

Speech/A Fungus A Mungus/Medi I
Black Christ Of The Andes
It Is Always Spring
Lord Have Mercy
My Mama Pinned A Rose On Me
Praise The Lord
Rosa Mae
Ella Mae
It's A Grand Night For Swinging

Rhapsody In Black - Virtuoso

For Abbey Lincoln

It's Magic
Straight Ahead
The People In Me
The World Falling Down

Abbey Singing Billie Even When She Blue
Talking At The Sun
Who Used To Dance
Wholly Earth
 It's Me Golden Lady
Over The Years
We Insist
Moon Faced And Starry Eyed
Music Is The Magic
It's Magic
Straight Ahead
The People In Me
The World Falling Down

Honeysuckle Rose
I Let A Song Go Out My Heart
Wake The Town
Tell The People
I Let A Song Go
Out Of My Heart
Out Into The Ether
Passed Through Veins
Wake The Town
Tell The People

Katherine Dunham taught us a Rhythm & We felt like Dancing

I feel like dancing
really dancing
like how they
used to do in Jamaica and Trinidad
and Haiti and Cuba
I feel like dancing
like really dancing
the anthropology of dance
the matriarch of black dance

Mambo
Mambo
Mambo
Mambo

star spangled rhythm

I feel like dancing
like really dancing
the anthropology of dance
the matriarch of black dance

Juba
Juba
Juba

you heard what happened in Brazil
Katherine Dunham danced america on the stage
showed all of its ugly parts
and they couldn't believe it
she danced american on stage
and they couldn't believe it
star spangled rhythm

the anthropology of dance
the matriarch of Black dance
star spangled rhythm

star spangled rhythm
star spangled rhythm
star spangled rhythm
star spangled rhythm
star spangled rhythm
star spangled rhythm
star spangled rhythm
star spangled rhythm
star spangled rhythm

the anthropology of dance
the matriarch of Black dance

Jump In The Sugar Bowl For Amina Claudine Myers

Amina Put One Hand On The Piano And I Thought About God A Warrior Of Our Dreams

So Much Money You Can Taste It
So Sweet
Mama Said It'll Rot Your Teeth
Run Yo Blood Up
Leave Yo Hands All Bloody
Curve Yo Back
Make You A Moon
All Around And Brittle
Yelling Into The Black Void Of Space

Anybody Out There
Sticky
Sweet
Aching
Molasses
Honey
So Sweet On Me Smile At Me So
So Sweet On Me Smiling
Meet Me On The Stoop Dressed Like Night Kissing Snow
So Sweet On Me
Must Be From Chicago
Or Harlem
Or Blackwell
Or Texas
So Sweet On Me

(Dial me up, I Know A Place, Kongo Sweet Revolutionary Lullaby)

My Thoughts Return To My You, My Lungs Return Back To The Coal Mine

Thankful For The Ghosts That BeBop The Future Friction We Almost Lost New York
Listening to the Ayler Brothers, I start thinking about the SOUNDS sounds that remind you of ya momma 'n em, sounds like love and madness entangled, sounds that collapse reality and open a portal to another dimension - see that's why the moon is smiling, the possibilities of sound, It's mothership, It's young Blues

Ask Larry Young
 Six views of the Blues *Moonscapes From the Mountain Top of Early Reflections*

Ask Bennie Maupin
 Natural illusions color schemes spirals waiting=g a view from the inside.

Enjoying the Views of Sound
Bobby Hutcherson & Beverly Watkins
Andrew Hill *& Eartha Kitt*
Sounds that be Dancing with Death
Passing Ships In The Night Sounds
Blue Black Eternal Spirit Sounds
From California with Love Sounds
Dreams come true Sounds
Divine Revelations Sounds
New Star Sounds

Ask Jimmy Smith
Chaos of Unformed Matter
Mars-Pluto War Cry of Love on the Battlefields of Life SOUNDS

Far Out Ratios

fire music, brass halo
junkie fried
rice and beans, double fried
skins and brushes
glass and crash
cymbal Muhal tri sphere
Baraka time codes
upside the head of a eastman score
in the wrong hands
must be left
must be used up american rag
copyright jasm inferno tent cities
skid row san francisco rag
laid and lied
vancouver budapest swinging
big guns brussels austin paris rag fire music
gut coal mine cave body lung pharaoh
woody shaw elevator out of town
far out ratios
Woody Shaw elevator out of town
Who's coming? Life got me going up & down

Time's pendulum

Classical Art

Southern Breeze
Max Roach Freeze
How Many Seconds Till They Come And Get Us
Who Coming With Me
Coltrane Shadow Boxing

Betty Carter Scatting Out Of The Chaos
Milford Drumming Through The Glitch
This Will Save Us Later
Quantum Futurist Behavior

Albert Ayler
You Don't Know What The Ghost Bring
Bird Set Loose In Our Dreams
This is Classical Art
Black Mass Nu Ark Screams
Rahsaan Roland Kirk Playing Everything At Once Cause We Be
Hearing Things
Seeing Spirits In The Dark Let Nina Simone Sing
*Cause It Don't Mean A Thing If It Ain't Got The **Blues***

[Drum Of Silence, The Circle Of The Instrument, The Leopard Lord]

Exodos (Ornette's Soulcraft)

Valaida Snow Timeless Jazz
Jazz Hounds Howling At The New Moon
Change Come On Right Now
Harlem Playgirls We can't wait
Sonny Rollins on sax its Work Time
Carmen McRae Now's The Time
Ray Brown Don't Forget The Blues
Paul Chambers This Is The Moment
We Need Rare Jazz With Soul Support
Kenny Dorham dancing at Soul Station
Hank Mobley writing Love Letters
Toni Morrison Thinking Of Home

Sun Ra Reminding Us Of The Magic Sun
Ornette Coleman Teaching Us To Break Though
Ornette Coleman Taking The Risk
Teaching Us To Say No
Teaching Us To Demand More
Saying Now Is The Time
The Shape Of Us To Come
Science Fiction
Free Music Dancing In Your Head
Because This World Right now Is A Crisis In All Languages
We Need A Love Call With Broken Shadows
Something Else, Of Human Feeling
A Relationship with Peace
Tomorrow Is The Question

Welcome To Tomorrow
Welcome To The Sound Museum
Where Would We Be
Without The Shape Of Jazz To Come
Where We Would Be?
Who would we be?

Bland Jazz America
No Sugar In Kool Aid
No Butter
No Hot Sauce
No Urgency
No Right Now

Ramblin

Music Of The Future
Calling All Lovers & Kind Spirits
Peace And Understanding To All
Before We Step In To An Unknown Portal
Before We Leave The Music Behind
& Catch Up With Our Spiritual Selves
Meet Our Ancestors
Start Chanting
Spelling Out The Alphabet In All Sound Languages
We Need A Love Call
Love Words
Body Meta
Angel Voice
Calling Out
When Will The Blues Leave
When Will The Blues Leave
Our Becoming Is Our Blessing

Transcending
Rewriting Laws
Casting Color On The Shadows Of America
The Skies Of America
The Many Hells Of America's tomorrow
We need A Love Call
Love Words
Body Meta
Angel Voice
Calling Out
Our Becoming Is Our Blessing

Times Square

Fast City Expressway
We All Have To Go Down That Road
We All Have A Home On That Rock
A Pilgrimage Through Sound
Transcendent Behavior
Sound Grammar
All My Life Through Sound
Speak My Own Language A Language Of Many Tongues
See It Is The Art Of Improvisers
To See And Seek Continually Inside Themselves
Inner Work
Inner World Prime Design Time Design
Time Reinvention
Let's Go Through The Colors
A New Vocabulary Of Wonder
Broadway Blues
The Garden Of Souls

Midnight Sunrise
Air Ship To Times Square
New York Right Now
Where City Soundscapes & Rural Sound Maps Collide
Rat Infested Rhythms
Evicted Operas
Good Mourning Heartbreak
Shot Down Gospels
We Going Down Old Moses
We Going Down Old Jeremiah

How could I forget?

The industry of sound
The devils disco

The ring of fire
The devil at the crossroad
The revoked cabaret card
The spotify ball & chain & plantation
The poisoned apple from amazon
The god algorithm + The space x contract + The pandora's box

Time Further Out

Air Mail
The First To Fly Rocket Starship
Spaceship Satellite Station
And Deliver The Message
Rain Sleet Summer Snow Circus Circus

Matana Roberts
Other Side Of The Coin Family Currency In Sound

Elaine Mitchener
Watching Because They Enjoy The Jazz Like They Enjoy The Sugar

Pat Thomas
Just To Play He Walked Country To Country White Suit Turnt Dusty Jazz
Re- Inventing Brilliance With Each Note

Henry Threadgill
Said Fuck These Labels Man I Don't Want You To Think Of Making
A Song
I Want You To Design A Future Sound World

Irreversible Entanglements
Let's Swing, We Entangled,
We Free, We Blue
We Homestead Grays,
Swinging Mean/Swinging Mad We Irreversible Sonic Entanglements

James Blood Ulmer
Back In Time.
There's No Escape From The Blues
Tales Of Ol Captain Black Forbidden Blues

Sonny Sharrock
Ask The Ages They Enter Dreams Like The Voices Of Sleeping Birds.

Old and New Dreams

A Sound, Known Like Don Cherry

See Our Birthday Is One Day Apart So
I Listen And Feel Like I Gotta Get Going
I Start Looking Around For Pen And Paper
Got Something To Write Down
Gotta Call A Few People
Need Someone To Play Bass

I need to know the codes
The Peace codes
The Healing codes
The Art of Sounding for peace
A Ritual
A Prayer
For peace
Sounding for peace
For peace we are healing
Dream-chasers for peace
Spiraling into the unknown for peace
Dream chasing for peace
Spiraling into the unknown
The heavy drum of silence
The circle of the instrument
The leopard's lure
We are sounding
We are Healing
Dream chasing
Soft landing
For Peace

Generational Griots & African Temporal Orchestration

Zora Neale Hurston
A Star Is Born
Notasulga Alabama

Life Story Collector
Eatonville Florida
Folklore Films and Fortunes
Anthropology Of Consciousness
Anthropology Of God's Science

It Won't Be Easy
From Haiti To Jamaica
An Ending Unfolding To Start Anew
Dorothy Masuka in Prayer
Octavia Butler leading Hoodoo rituals
Bobbi Humphrey on Bamboo Flutes
Sarah Vaughan Morning Hymn
Patrice Rushen on theremin
Shirley Horn burning down Dixieland
Pops Foster's dreaming Boogie Woogie
Hollywood Africans entering Gothic Futurism
Nation of Gods and Earth's Migrations
Terri Lyne Carrington on Drums
Joseph Bologne Beginning
Voltaire Exploding
Scott Joplin Continuing
Zora Neale Hurston Resurrected
Sonia Sanchez Composing
Alice Walker Conducting
Angela Davis Sounding the Trumpets.
Toni Morrison Writing New Bibles From Heaven

Can The Saints Hear The Word?
Will They Come Marching In?

Indigo Blue (Sea Island Pure). 2016. Courtesy Alison Saar.

CLASSICAL ECONOMICS

Red Notes Black Rhythms Slavery's Echo in Black American Classical Economics

People & Places Orchestral Temporal Echoes economics 3009391 Allargando 1 01 eco 1 economics 1 The Financial Fabric Adagio3 008jd9n Chronicles of America Tonal Equality Dualities in U.S. Equations economics and Tones Racial Metrics 11 0 1 economics economics Affettuoso 6p3541 Oppression, Culture, Tone, America, Verse, Equality 6n3541 A piacere 4u economics American Inequalities 32700bd8 Capitalism and the Evolution Classical Economics 101: Adagietto econ 0 Abbellimenti economic 094b 005 FUTURE PLANTATIONS X OPPRESSION OLYMPICS 22298737 Agitato economics AccelerandoTHIS SECTION IS CALLED CLASSICAL ECONOMICS BECAUSE TRUTH INVESTS MONEY AT A BANK CALLED DEATH

Classical Economics 1

William Levi Dawson & Florence Price
Sierra Leone Dreams from Little Rock to New England
Nathaniel Dett
Our cup has runneth over
But we not done troubling the spirit
William Grant Still
Our Hope Of The Night
Compost Dixie Philharmonic
The Ordering Of Moses
Sanford Allen & Marian Anderson saying
Listen To The Lambs
Don't Be Weary Traveler
We Almost Home

What Is American Music?

American Music is
Yoruba Drum Language
Bunce Island Djembe
Tchaikovsky Black Metal Black Hole
Symphony No.1 At The Move Bombing
Rural Symphonies in Mississippi Cotton Fields
Strauss /Electrofied at the Baltimore County Jail
Hamid Drake's drum kit on the Banks of Jordan
Marion Brown with Oliver Lake composing at Pruitt-Igoe
Treaty of Dancing Rabbit Creek
Schoenfield Folk Memories of War
Sun Ra Reminiscing In Tempo Black Feeling
George Lewis Chicago Trombone Realities
36 Chambers of Wu Tang Clan
The Ragtime of J Dilla
Reich Verses Eastman at Cabrini Green
Zulu Warrior Battle Cry
Roy Ayers In the Sunshine
Piano Sonata No.32 Dreams & Nightmares
Sam Rivers thinking of Oceans
Piano Variations of the Sahara
The Church of Hugh Masekela

Sonny Rollins & Miles Davis in Love
Time traveling Booker Little listening to Miles Davis
Slave Labor Camp Songs
Penitentiary Work Songs
Chevalier De Saint - Georges vs Mozart
Celia Cruz laughing in Cuba
James Baldwin writing about revolution
Pheeroan Aklaff in Watts
Debussy Playing for Ghost in Savannah Georgia
Georgia Mass Choir at Fannie Lou Hammer's Funeral
Bird Songs at Rucker Park
Patti LaBelle at the Apollo
Leontyne Price at Carnegie Hall
David Murray & Saul Williams in Brooklyn writing poetry
Bill Dixon all by Himself in a Baptist Church
The Underground Resistance in Detroit
New York Art Quartet meeting Fats Waller in New Orleans
Margaret Bonds Troubling the water
Julius Eastman Staying on it safe within
Douglas Ewart with Irreversible Entanglements In Minneapolis
Yusef Lateef Awakening
James P. Johnson at the piano
Blind Boy Fuller smashing a guitar
Nikki Giovanni playing synthesizers
Big Joe Turner singing in the AME choir
Helen Humes 1913 Louisville Kentucky
Chickasaw Language
American music is
Black Swan Records
Amtrak Underground Railroad Blues
Noble Sissle
Mohawk
Osage
Andy Razaf & William Parker
Billy Harper & Big Joe Williams
Tulsa 1921
It sounds like
Somebody Blew Up America
Francis Johnson & Howard Swanson
Red Summer 1919

Roscoe Mitchell Painting
Burning Spear Soundsystem
It sounds like
The First Slave Ship
Fletcher Henderson verses Bix Beiderbecke
Hubert Harrison & Harlem hellfighters
The Weary Blues
Sounds Like
Ron Carter & Florence Mills
Moorish Temple Harlem Stride Style
Henry Burleigh & Zenobia Perry
The Cherokee Phoenix
The treaty of Greenville
Edward Bland & George Walker
Amiri Baraka Blues People
Julia Perry & Dorothy Rudd Moor
Harry Freeman & Ulysses Kay
Black Seminoles & Choctaw
Art Tatum & The Belleville Three
Undine Moore & The Famous Flames
Toni Cade Bambara
African American Inventions
Gloria Nayler
Bodega BeBop
June Jordan
It Sounds Like
The Georgia Mass Choir
Jesus on the cross
Bernie Worrell & Don Pullen
Black Belt Bible Belt Blues
KoKo Taylor & Gil Scott Heron
East St. Louis Massacre

It sounds like us beginning to remember

Who and what is American music?
Who gets to decide?
Who knows how to listen?
Who taught you how to listen?
What do we sound like?

CLASSICAL ECONOMICS ll - *Ritardando*

[$ Oil Blood Bank Of American Dreams States, Cotton Dust Dollars Under God We Breathe]

Night Thief
The Distant Colonial Gaze

They stole my sound
I saw them
Laughing looking up on the hill
Last sunday
Now they on the minstrel circuit
Doing my dance
Singing my song
With no trace of ME
Racist Capital Entertainment Of Historical Mocking
Algorithmic Laughing A.I. Generated Ghost Currency
NO Memory
NO Past
NO Future
NO History

King Cotton
John Sousa
Lucid Dreams
Wallace Willis
The Angels are Coming
Wait til I put on my Crown
The Angels are Coming
I Don't Feel No Ways Tired
The Angels are Coming
I Want All My Stuff Back
The Angels are Coming
I Want To Be Ready
The Angels are Coming
Get on board Children
The Angels are Coming
Steal Away Steal Away
The war machine has started again

Burning Headline Live Smoke

I Ask Myself What Am I Doing Here?
In The Ruins
In The Aftermath
In The Graveyard
In The Church Of A Confused God
A Confused Statehood
An Unknown Oz

30,000 By 1860
182,566 San Antonio
$800 US Dollars
$2000 US Dollars
Year 1850
East Texas Forest
Galveston Island
Rio Grande
Fort Bend
Colorado County
Army Of Texas
Post Civil War
Brazoria County
Texas Democratic Party
11,323 In Texas
Greene -Dewitt Colonies
Cameron County
Carry My Soul Up Yonder
Yes My Soul, Yes Right Now
Storm Weather Hurricane
Ol Red River Flooding Again
I Mean Remembering
That Endless Chant
Shadow Of Bitter Earth
I'll Be Visiting Soon
On This Side Or The Other
Blue Spirits Freddie Hubbard

Betty Bebop & The Black Saints

This One Is For The Black Saints Together In Holy Sound.
Sound The Blueprint Of Creation.
I Know It's Possible Because I Seent It.
United
Intertwined
The Foundation
The Foundation Of A Possible History

We Had To Go Through it
The Flooding of Red River
Dixie In Technicolor
Paramount
Riverboat
The New Minstrel
Live At The Opera House
Starring Daniel Decatur Emmett
Now Tell Me Who Had To Use The Back Door,
Walk The Footsteps Of Atom
Particle Physics
Made Sure That You Saw/See The Noose
1920 2020 1820 1420 Hospitality
1889 Aberdeen Mississippi
1894 Palestine Alabama
1934 Newton Texas
1917 England Arkansas
10,000 in Paris Texas

We Continue To Go Through It
Wading
The Break
The Portal
The Final Frontier
The Wake

Burning *Headline Holy Smoke*

Satan, your kingdom must come down
Go tell it on the mountain - Children, Go where I send thee
& Revolt

Indigo Bled English
Spanish Dye Lies
French Cotton King Dutch Sugar Cane
Duke Of York Dressed In White New Christians
Barbadian Rum At Death Camp Nevis
Portuguese Shipwrights
Denmark Sea Captains at the New World Navigators School
Old World Roman Empire Drugs
Whitehaven Ships crashing into each other
Is this the New World?
Is this the Future?
Is this Death Country?

ADVERTISEMENTS

20,000 acres of plantations IN EXCHANGE FOR JOHN
GLADSTONE, THOMAS PARR, RICHARD WYATT, PETER
BECKFORD, JOHN LOK & SAMUEL GREG

£90,000 IN EXCHANGE FOR THE ROYAL AFRICA
COMPANY, TISSINGTON HALL, BELMONT ESTATE &
QUARRY BANK MILL, BLAISE CASTLE, THE HOUSE OF
COMMONS IN 1833

II

Peculiar Institutions Peculiar Happenings (Who builds death like this?)
British West Indies
The Royal Navy
Dutch West India Company
Red Sea Slave Trade
The Atlantic
Niger River
Sierra Leone Company
African Colonization Expedition Cape Coast
Bissagos Islands Village Of The Maroons
Benkos Bioho
BEWARE Vreedenhoop Plastic City
BEWARE Dominica & Queen's Square
BEWARE Yorkshire & Gresham Street

Death & The Invisible Powers
#$ Extends Into The Invisible World Of Spirits

Act 1 - THE KING'S HISTORY
Symphony no. 1 vs Serenade No. 13 in G Major, K 525

Street paved with West Indian Gold
We're on our way to buy ourselves a seat in Parliament

(The $uperfund/FUND$ ITE of $lavery are everywhere)

Act 2 THE PLAN I AMERIGO
Fantasie Nègre (in E Minor)

1830
India might be a replacement for Africa

Act 3 SOUTH CAROLINA
Fantasie nègre (in G Minor)

(A Lord's Prayer)

Dollar Cotton
Forgive us our Debt$
Our $in = Debt
Our $ervice = $lavery

X + ($ilent $am) = 20th century

Act 4 STONO RIVER REVOLUTION
Nocturne Op. 9 No. 2

What Always
What Everywhere
What By All
Is Held To Be True
Even If It's A Lie
A Dead Lie In A Grave
$Tone Age Economics 101
Labor Death Camp News & Wedding Invitations

1500 Haiku

The birth of angels temporal agents of jesus provider of air

1500 (Desk/Death Notes)

Bridgewater Canal
Manchester
Liverpool Scared of its own reflection
Leeds
Bolton Remembering 1807 with zero capacity
Oldham Cotton Mills
Halifax Death Camp
Severn
Trent River
Grand Junction Canal
Salthouse Dock
George's Dock
King's Dock
Queens Dock
St. Paul Church
St. John Church
St Thomas Church
The Exchange
Three African Heads
Six Ropes

The Exchange
Three African Heads And Six Ropes
The Birth Of Angels, Temple Agents Of Jesus
Now Tell Me Who Provides The Air?
Dollar Cotton

Financial Fabrics Hang In Virginia
Metal Talks
Wood Talks
We Smell What Is Certain
We See Bits Of Beauty
We Wish We Could Hold A Little Longer

But Know The Reality
Know The Obsession
The Lust
The Thirst
What Comes Next
The Horns
The Dogs
The Flashes Of Hell
The Salt In Wounds
The Heads Along The Highways
(Capitalist Crescendos Slavery's Silence In The Mouth Of America)
The Madness
Decades Of Madness
Too Big To Comprehend
Just The Thought
Break Hearts Into A Billion Bits Of Sand
Dusted Conclusions

Harewood

Close To Each Other Like Books On A Shelf
Death Destinations

Counterpoint

1 Million in the West Indies
3 Thousand hours a minute

Mansfield Slave Labor Camp Plantation
Georgetown County, South Carolina
Magnolia Grove Slave Labor Camp
Stagville (plantation) Durham County, North Carolina
Greensboro, Alabama
Wallblake House, The Valley, Anguilla
Valley of the Sugar Mills
San Luis, Santa Rosa
Macon County Named After The Last Of The Romans
Leeuwenhof Cape Town, South Africa
Rosewood, Jefferson County, Mississippi
The Hermitage, Davidson County, Tennessee

Three thousand hours in a minute.
Three thousand hours in a minute,
just to get over the Bridgewater Canal.
just to get over Trent River
George's Dock
The King's Dock
The Queen's Dock

Is this the future?
Is this a looping war?
Is this religion?

I ain't heard No prayer coming out of Saint Paul's Church, or Saint
John's Church, or Saint Thomas Church. No Vibrato Or Tremolo.

Negative One BC – 1BC
(the day jazz decided to live.. after everything america had done to her)

Fisk University
Nashville 1866
Jubilee Day
October 6th 1971
Leviticus Chapter 25
1871 Liverpool
1872 The White House
1873 for Queen Victoria
See I've Been In The Storm

Ragtime Rag
Maple Leaf Rag
Original Rag
Mississippi Rag
Too Much Jelly Roll
Too Much Memphis Blues
Bolden Armstrong
Cakewalk Havana Kongo
Hot Jazz Betsy And Duke
Dusk Jazz Musky Lester Bowie
New Ark Screams Of Justice
Sun Ra Halo Roscoe Chi-Congo
Mississippi To East Texas
Deep Grass Swamp Rag
Calloway Big Band Barbados Hip Swinging
Hands Clapping Against The Chest Of Jefferson County
Louisiana
Mr. Tambo & Mr. Bones
Old Zip Coon
Banjo Bones
Ivory Tambourine
Tennessee
Fisk Jubilee Singers
Late Eighteen Hundred
Authentic
A Breath In Rhythm
Without A Time-Piece

Ragtime Rag
Deep In The Wilderness Of Our Minds
All Ours
Innovation
And Here Come Ol Minstrel
Painted Face
New Age Capitalists
New Age Oppressors
In Liberty And Justice For All
A Trillion Dollars Later
The Clock Still Ticks Unpaid Labor

2 Aftermath Echo

Copycat Pop Minstral
K - Pop - Afro - Pop - RnB - Pop - Rock - Pop
All Pretending To Be The Root
End Up Twisted Plastic Inside Some Great Blue Whale

Artificial Music Lab Created For An Automatic Audience
Audience Of No Memory
Audience Of Regulated Heart Rhythms
Audience Of Male Aggression
Audience Of Sex Lust And Jealousy
Audience Of Illusions
The Clock Still Ticks
Broken Dreams And Deals With The Devil
Record Contracts
Publishing Contracts
Time Contracts
Death Contracts
Blood Contracts
Sharecropping Contracts
Bills Of Sale
License Agreements
Promissory Notes
Dead Trees Dead Ends
Roots Stop Growing
Start Decomposing
Then They Pour Salt

Apprentice Haiku For Elizabeth Broadway - *Ostinato*

just couldn't let her go tied ship to tongue heart to devil god of slavery

Le Hours Le Law
time is a quarantine device

temporal ownership
6am to sunset
got me a timepiece
the old ball and chain
drag me everywhere i go
doin time
wages of the tardy

Got me a timepiece,
The old ball and chain.
Drag me everywhere I go.
From the valley of the sugar mills all the way down to Rosewood,
Jefferson County, From Mississippi to Magnolia Grove to Georgetown
County, South Carolina to The Mansfield Slave Labor Camp
British Time Militia
Heavy clocks in Anguilla
Broken Clocks Bermuda
Cayman Islands Clock and Bell
Montserrat Clock and Whip
Dead Clocks in Turks and Caicos
The invasion of Jamaica
Windward Maroons Revolt
By 1650 37,000 in Barbados
Uprising in Hispaniola
Port De Paix
A curse for the Earl of Portland
Age of Absolution
1940 The Duke of Windsor is a clone

Dismantle the timelocks
alla breve

Zong 55 Thousand Haiku - *Lento*

How pure can you be white knight of death and color, caveman in latin

Zong 55 Thousand
A thousand lightyears inside - Atonality

Coast of West Africa
1781 September (6) Six
Four hundred seventy towards Jamaica
One hundred eighty four dead

dirge
prelude to a massacre
no concern
we have insurance

cargo
less than human
the business of

death &
whiteness &
industry &
empire &

personality &
cult &

temporal enclosures
& retrograde

Faithful Memorial Song
(song in the key of death) Battaglia

I Went To Denton County Courthouse And Died And Died I Tell You

I Went To Morgan County Courthouse And Died And Died I Tell You

I Went To Lauderdale County Santa Rosa And Died And Died I Tell You

I Went To Hale County Courthouse And Died And Died I Tell You

I Went To Madison County Courthouse And Died And Died I Tell You

I Went To Lawrence County Courthouse And Died And Died I Tell You

I Went To Summers County Courthouse And Died And Died I Tell You

I Went To Christian County Courthouse And Died And Died I Tell You

I Went To Lee County Courthouse And Died And Died I Tell You

I Went To Hood County Courthouse And Died And Died I Tell You

I Went To Marion County Courthouse And Died And Died I Tell You

I Went To Tallahatchie County Courthouse And Died And Died I Tell
You

I Went To Charleston County Courthouse And Died And Died I Tell You

I Went To Sussex County Courthouse And Died And Died I Tell You

I Went To King And Queen County Courthouse And Died And Died I
Tell You

I Went To Richmond County Courthouse And Died And Died I Tell You

I Went To Ellis County Courthouse And Died And Died I Tell You

and somehow I still ain't free, can't pay my bill of rites/rights & wrongs
still on/for sale auction block encores

Dinner at the Demby plantation (slave labor camp)

1
nathan mayer rothschild
charles the second
the devil
richard pennant
the lascelles family
24 slave labor camps
21 ships
grenada
6 sugar plantations
6 hundred enslaved
sugar up 200 percent
sugar and slavery
the heywood brothers
2 burning bibles
sugar from the west indies
cotton from america
blood from bristol
mix it all together we get an atomic bomb

2
after dinner
industrial empires pizzicato

in the company of the isles of america
war of the grand alliance
guadeloupe
martinique
Grenada
royal african company
crown colony plantation society
In saint lucia with thomas warner
and here come the knights of malta
with the treaty of madrid
of utrecht
of paris
of death

3
dirt hands
how come we can't remember
building the railroads
the churches
the financial revolution
the empire
the up and down
the going
the peace out
the love below
the jive
the ages
the bebop
the drag
the heat fire the flame
the exchange
the future
the smokehouse
the spring house
the juke joint
the blues
the praise house
the chicken house
the tobacco barn
the graveyard
the black star line
the wash house
the milk house
the sugar mill
the farmhouse
the overseer house
the sugarcane barn
the upland cotton mill
the sea land cotton mill
the cotton gin house
the chapel of the cross

the highways
the revenge of queen anne
the enterprise
the second line

A Dream? I Remember A Nightmare
A skywalk
moor archway
afrofuturist architecture
red line/black line
village slum
spatial other
magnum opus
ritual fire
Kongo caves
limestone kingdoms
hologram clay suns
silver chariots
lynched angels from 1590
crossing borders with a roman priest
inner eyes
In the red
Praying for the death of napoleon
generational eyes
In the black
lace skirts
silk stocking
young men/old boys
fractured reptilian hearts
High Heel masculinity
High Hell patriarchy

(notes from the kitchen)
slave trade > modern banking > royal bank of scotland >
Insurance fraud > bank of china > city of london > (coffee mills) > manchester
arkwright 150 years / northwest 1960 /1807 slave trade act / north hampton /
15 million pounds

august 3rd 1835 holiday for bankers /Atlantic Ocean > Portugal > Spain > France
Belle Vue Farm x Oakington Farm x Swan Harbor Farm
Sharecropper insurance > Rococo > Reconstruction > Black Codes (Amistad) x jp morgan & co >

(notes from the shotgun house)
100 thousand + enslaved in Ghana x Wels plantation/West Indies
compensation company
London Virginia company /New France /12 billion pounds / 17 billion
pounds / 20 billion pounds

Inverted Memorials

I'm a long way from home
I feel like a Motherless Child
Won't be long now
Something coming
Freedom or Death
North or South
Factory Fields or Tobacco fields
Political War Economies

Histories of the minute
Sun-rise to Sun-down
And sometimes No Sun at all
Just the Night holding Light So tight feels like it may cry
May Lightning/Thunder if you ask why

Is this the end of history?

Asking Africans in Genoa
Asking Africans in Venice
Is this the end of history?
In Lagos Portugal following Henry the Navigator
Henry Morton Stanley Another death agent
The Senegal River
Mountains of the moon
Pratt Street
Adams Street
Cherry street
Shockoe Bottom
The Franklin and Armfield Office
Price, Birch & Co
Alexandria Virginia
283 Duke St.
Polk County
Eureka Springs
Glass Negatives
Brazzaville
July 1891 Tanzania
The white fathers, the so called missionaries of Africa
Is this death Becoming?

Triangle Haiku - Contralto

the port remembers the slow walk into the void washing away the blood

Back/Black On Base

Look at all these (yt) women building statues for the confederacy.
No cau$e, just cau$e lost co$t ideology

All Alone
(Left the labor camp for the union, for the north, for the lie and I'll do
it again)

Alone at Fort Lee with the children of the confederacy
(Did daddy fight like they told him to? Did he flee north?)

Alone at Fort Gordon with the sons of confederate veterans
(Future nothing Wet future nothing but Blood in Texas)

Alone at Fort Bragg with the united daughters of the confederacy
(They Spit and Spat and Spit Spat Venom in Canada)

Alone at Fort Polk with the ladies memorial association of Gainesville
 (No rose No throne No scent No hue in Florida)

Alone at Fort Rucker with the prattville dragoons
(a myth and a bible in Philadelphia)

Alone at Fort Sumter
(best stay woke no rest in Charleston)

Alone at Fort Henry
(working on a memory erasing device)

Alone at Fort Donelson, Fort Nassau, Fort Monroe
(haunted by ghosts from Barbados)

Extraction of Blackness
 - Question - When will they be full/Fulfilled by war?

The Gospel & The Blues
I'm leaving off the banks of jordan but they still trying to chalk line me

Early Moan Casted Upon The Fire Of Our Crumbling Fortunes
In A Million Tongues We Pray.
You can't firebomb a communal sound.
You can't evict holy ghost hoodoo spirits already let loose.

St. Bartley Primitive Baptist Church
Faith Congregational Church
Pleasant Green Missionary Baptist Church
Mount Carmel United Methodist Church
First African Baptist Church
16th Street Baptist Church
Mt. Pisgah AME Church
Abyssinian Baptist Church
St. Philip's Protestant Episcopal Church
Mother African Methodist Episcopal Zion Church
Mother Bethel Ame Church
African Episcopal Church Of St. Thomas
First African Presbyterian Church
Springfield Baptist Church
Mother Emanuel AME Church
Mason Temple Church of God in Christ
Liberty Elm AME Church
St. James AME Church

We Hear You

50

The Night Battles
Dripping Jazz
The Black Atlantic
Balancing The Lopsided Load

Some Wanted To Make A Complete Break From The Past
Hang Up All The Cotton
Hang Without A Rope
With Demons And Devils
Embody Colonial Memories

51

I Am Because You Are
A Shadow
A Breath
A Personality
A Mirror Quartered By The Crossroads
I Used My Four Eyes
Disappeared When I Went To Sleep
Disappeared For Two Days
I Could Not Speak Until Tomorrow

52

Crimes Of The Dream World
The Work Of Memory
Body Of Remembrance
Multiple Timelines

Musical Time
The Art Of Time
Special Relativity
A Paradox of Color

53

Blackface Democracy
Legacy Congress

Slave House Senate
Outhouse Campaign
Chicken House Humanity

54

Amazing Grace Aretha Franklin
James Cleveland Handclap Across The Face
Let's Clap The Night Away
Shirley Caesar Lay Hands On
Make The Devil Pay

55

From The Womb Of Iron & Gold
Speak The Tongues Of Afrika
Drums And Shadows
Moonlight Ritual
Light Matters
Trails of Light
Invisible Light
Catching the Light Spirit
Parallel Universe Travel
The Peripheral

56

Old Time Molasses
Elegy For
Neoclassicism
Libretto
Eye And Mind
Brilliant Disguises

57

Theology of light
Workers and worshipers
Journey into gravity
Is this spacetime?
Is this God time?

Is this storytime?
The legend of Ra
Genesis
The evolution of time

58

Our nation's archive
From small town to oil empire
Different mirrors
Survival strategies
A long long way from home
Sound travel studies
Black woman temporal

59

We all gotta travel down that lonesome road
Backdoor The metropolitan opera house 1883

60

A poetic meditation for the fire of sound
For the love of you
The sweat of a dream
Hanging over me
Singing sweet blues
Sweet indigos
Summer breeze
All the while in this cycle of terror
BUT they can't hold no dream captive
and they can't beat imagination out of the mind
As long as you got a heart beating you got music
and don't nobody own the melody but you

Classical Rage

Seeking the origin of music
Bird taught us to sing
Bird set loose in our dreams
Nina Simone asked for our participation
Did she know?
we would lose
our memories
our mind
the fire in our hearts?

How many more years in this waste?
plantation mosh pit
jazz overload
theory and nostalgia
a sickness
a home sick
searching for borders
a need to belong
a social construct
too many futures for sell
souls for sell
death for sale
rebirth for sell

check the calendar
the sex and jazz in the city
in the country
low county
dig up the earth
up from the mud
cover our secrets
hide our memories
the jasm
the sex
the ritual
zip yo lips
dont hum a word
on the banks of jordan

in the swamp
on the dock
sweet tide
ticking us out
the blinding gaze
the pulse of the internet
consumers with no product
just plastic dust in the wind
(once at last a blues or was it jazz upon a time?)

Dear Jupiter

It's all chaos
blinding green lights
red smoke nightmares
screaming exit wounds of grief
I am 400 acres out
4 light minutes moon blood cycles away

stormy weather oh my grief
stormy weather
the rain the rain
the rain echos
didn't it rain echos
didn't the rain run back in time
didn't the wind make the rain reverse
didn't it rain, our roots exposed
didn't we sing the gospel
felt the hoodoo ghost
rode the midnight train for light hours
from heaven to hell
from tallahassee to oslo

Dear Saturn

they are pulling up all the roots
gathering for the butcher
dinner table of forgotten truths
its slow burning

slow gut stew
bland jazz europe
white ivory lies
virtual hills real estate
internet state of minds
good riddance folks
duds and dims & wanna be light works
it's all here
underneath our feet
the day of the dead

it's chaos
blinding lights
red nightmares
screaming grief
i am out
light cycles away

Just Ask The Blues
Ask Leon Thomas From East St. Louis
Ask Ferdinand Joseph Lamothe

They want to regulate our minds
You know
They ain't never studied
What we did
What I did
The science
The ritual
The invention
It's just cheap nostalgia

classical rage
no smiles allowed
no feelings allowed
no movement - no reaction to the rhythm
private sex minds
god & priest veil
classical sonic vortexes choir & strings from 1850

Traditional Blues Economics

1

Here Comes That
Boil Weevil
Eating Through The
Cotton States
Eating Through The
Cotton Belt
Old Cotton Full Of Money
Here Comes That
Boil Weevil
Must Be Sent From God

2

Missionary
Please
Please
Don't Need No More
Christianity

Five Churches In One Village
All Roman Catholic
How Many In Uganda?

I Bear De Wait
I Bear De Weights
I Bear De Mental
I Bear De Metal

Missionary
Missionary

(I Sung The Song /I Drunk The Wine/ I Dined On The Flesh)

HUMAN RESOURCES

Once They
Re-Map Re Grid Rewire the Land
Then they
Re-Map Re Grid Rewire the People
 the Robots - Genetic Architecture /Agriculture
Eugenic Housing Agencies/Authorities

Environmental protection agency please explain who is, what is,
considered to be the environment again!

Something in the Air Poison
Something in the Ground Poison
For Centuries
In our Neighborhood
Scared to Breathe
Scared to Walk
Scared to Talk
Scared to Eat

Gonna have to fly away
Gonna grow some wings early in the morning
Early in the morning
Follow that north star to another place
Far from here
Far From the buildings pumping smoke
Far from the school in the land field

Gonna have to fly away
Early in the morning

Chains and Capital

1

They keep looking up at the open sky
Waiting for the end of time
Waiting for the age of never
Death against life in the computer age
Light against death in the computer age
Big dreams in the computer age
Coded dreams in the computer age
Knowing machines Biochemistry
Squeezing time Virtual time
Out of shape shifting pockets
The Banks of man
Trust fund hands across America

2

Somebody Blew Up America
He taught us how to build Revolutionary Plays
Set stages for Revolutionary Acts
The Essence Of Spatial Reparations

3

The European ku klux Slave Ship
The Black Belt
The Bible belt
The Hauluijah highway
The Fire cross
The Fire bomb
The devils hoodoo

4

Now that we found love what are we going to do
Held up in Harlem
Street Dreams Crooklyn Dodgers

If this world was mine Our Mothers singing Luther
The Magic would come on home
Teddy Pendergrass singing Feel the Fire
African Rhythms Talking
Telling tales and warm memories
Drum language
Drum tongue wagging
Come in the drum house
Don't make me wait

5

Old Bop
Old Rhythm
Old Time
Old Future
Old Stuff
Let's Call It Art
Black Magic
Heathens And Space/Time Projection
35th Reunion Freebop Now
Malachi Thompson
Hugh Ragin
When Sun Ra Gets Blue

I Plan To Stay A Believer
Africa Revisited
Knowledge Of Self It's Nation Time

6

you better hold ur secrets
you better hold ur traditions
you better hold ur dreams tight
because the vultures are ready
high above all of us
in the costume of william penn

ben franklin
girard
In the south they got ice
in the west they got a myth
in the north they take you out of ur neighborhood one by one
and sell you to the highest bidder

7

Henry Morton Stanley dressed as the devil
Arcade du Cinquantenaire
Ivory Talks
Rubber Talks
Money Talks
Fredericksburg, Virginia
Stay away from Whitehall Street
Alexandria Price Birch & Co

8

19 sticks of dynamite
21 pieces of glass in her face
Mortar in skull
4 little girls

Bible study
A setting for a race war
Before we die let's pray

A rock that will not roll
Where you gonna run to on judgment day?
Best stay woke eyes open

White Lion & The Treasurer

Prayed too late
It's gonna rain again
See you in the rapture
Saints hold on
You know not the hour
Born ten thousand years ago
From spirituals to swing
Mbuki Mvuki

Mooringsport Louisiana
Imperial Farm Sugar Land Texas
10 miles from Texarkana
Wenn ich bei dir sein kann
April 9th 1931

We danced in joy Shook off the gaze The brutality And build our
own Church School new morning
Newtown
Rentiesville
Stonetown
Nicodemus
Galveston
Blackville
Garcia Real de Santa Teresa de Mose
Africatown
Veracruz
Quindaro
Blackamoors
Angola
San Juan
Palace of Placentia
Saxe-coburg-gotha
Edisto Island

Living Below the Line
Court house yard lexington kentucky

Syracuse
Birmingham
Lake Charles
Springfield
Albany
Gainesville
Hartford
Decatur
Milwaukee
Lawton
Barre
Baltimore
Jonesboro
Memphis
Bowling Green
St Joseph
Providence
North Charleston
Flagstaff
Sunrise Manor
Richmond
Lawrence
Wilmington
10 Million Children
100 Million Children
How Many Children?
How Many Can't..?
How Many Almost..?
How Many Never Again?
We Keep Forgetting
We Kept Forgetting
Collecting We Forgots & We Forgets
Lost From Mind

We must remember the children
Fire bombed and Gunned down
Blindfolded executed at the edge of existence

Who else has Ghost currency?
Who else has a Flag sewn in blood?
Who else B flat?
Who else is a Lying rag?
Is it Mozart's 5th or Juilliard's lung?
Who's Coming?
Is it Sambo's Gun or Mary's Myth coming to carry us over?

Cultural Reset
A Loop
Experiencing Time
Brass
Bells
Whips
Chains
Branding Time
A For Atom
C For Confederacy
The Flow Of Time
Civil War Time Lag
Time Madness
Time Economic Bias

Are You An Illusion?
Time Passing Clocks Of Long Yesterdays
Something Don't Seem Right
Something Don't Make Sense
How Come We Still Waiting
Doing Digital Time
Bankrupt Algorithms
Debating Whether We Should Go Back And Help The Past
How Dare We Truth Or Dare Our Way Into the Last Laugh
Into Oblivion
Into Invisibility
Checked Out States Of Mind
States Of Being Retro Mania
The Entangled Love And Hate Of The African Woman
Love Her Milk But Hate Her Existence

Red Notes Black Rhythms
Slavery's Echo in Black American Classical Economics

The Sale Is Up
Auction Block Crescendos
I'm On Time

Sold And Paid For
How Disgusting
America

Running Away
From Its Forever
Permanent Stain

How Disgusting
The Benefactors
With Every Red Note

Bankrupt Humanity
Cultural Mis-Understandings
Miseducation of Truth
And What Are We Left With?

The Echo

The Alarming Echo

The Etched Echo

The Echo Symphony No.5 in C minor Death Echo
The Defining Echo
The Blinding Echo

The Echo The Echo Of Slavery The Echo
The Echo The Detuned Echo Of Slavery
The Echo The Echo The Echo The Echo Symphony No. 6 The
Money
The Echo Symphony No. 3 The Echo The Echo The Echo The Echo
The Echo The Echo The Echo The Echo The Echo Symphony No. 2
The Echo The Echo The Everlasting Echo The Echo The Echo The
Echo
The Echo Requiem

Black Snake Blues. 1994. Courtesy Alison Saar.

AMERICAN LEGATO

American Equations In Black Classical Music

Inner Outcomes 339330 Harmonizing Unseen Equations 339330
3344400 003333 Equations 3331 Black Equations American Tones
three equations 3 three equations Ink and Ivory 0 Arithmetic of Color
three equations equations333001 Equations in Musical Verses 33300
Equations in the Temporal Realm of Orchestration 0000000 Equations
The Inner Outcomes 98736198490 Reading the future 96958322003
Hold a mirror up to the moon 727 Water mirror spirits 049000000
Sacred mirrors broken 00190010 In Order To be whole again 3940
MIRROR LIBRARIES 000204097 Full with the moon 25869700020

American Equations In Black Classical Music

Before 1900
Cold World
Cold War
Cold Heart
Low Temperatures
Low Vibrations
Frozen
Unmoved
No Fire
Cold Case
Cold Blooded
Cold Sweat
Cold Call
Nobody On The Other Line
Nobody Picking Up
No Help On The Way
5 seconds Between Heaven and Colonialism
One Day We Will All Be Ghosts

After 1900
All In A Line
Fire Away
Fire Eaters
Fired Up
Butane
Propane
Class F
Class B
Sun Lady & Ra
Burning Up
Broken Fire Extinguisher
Firetruck Aint Coming
Fireman Ain't Coming
No Fire Escape
No Fire Drill
No Chill
10 Seconds Between Hell And Industry
One Day We Will Make It Out

University Equations

Who Told These Students That One Day They Would Be Masters?

SELF Visits & Experiments

<u>Visit #1</u>

What sounds bring profit?
How much was made from the sound of war?
The sound of suffering?
The sound of sex?
The sound of the internet?
The sound of you for sale?

<u>Experiment #1</u>

For 24 hours
Do not create or listen to any new <u>sounds</u>
Only collect the sounds of your childhood
Write them <u>out</u>

<u>Studio Visit #2</u>

Make a list of all the things you say to yourself while <u>creating</u>
Who taught you those words?
What root is it tongue tied with?
Who are you speaking to?
Who has the privilege to understand you?

<u>Experiment #2</u>

Look up the etymology of the following <u>words</u>
Sound
Noise
Silence
Create new definitions for <u>each</u>

Studio Visit #3

What does your inner world sound like?
What does your heart sound like?
Can you recreate the inner sounds of you?
What will the outcome be?

Experiment #3

When waking spend the first 10 minutes in silence
Write out the sounds you hear including the thoughts and bodily rhythms

Studio Visit #4

Does the sound of nature fit into the genre?
What does light sound like?
How can we listen to nature without our ears?
Does the human gaze prescribe sound to the beauty of nature?

Experiment #4

Day 1

Find a tree - compose a song for the tree
 - sit next to the tree for 1 hour then compose a song dedicated to the tree
Go home practice

Day 2

Go back to the tree and perform the composition

The Texas Equations

1

Stars Like Fire, Like Metal, Like Smoke

Texas, You Better Get Your Gay Boots On
Set Up Your Oil Suckers
Your Ole Lone Stars And That Deep Poison Hop Juice
You Better Get Your Fire Suit On
Burn Yo Way Out Of Here

2

Pop Stars Drink Whole Milk

The Cowboys Dance Around The Fire
The Cowboy Dances Around The The Burning Body
The Cowboy Dances Death
Desert Bones Devil Dance
Watch Them Ride Off Into The Future
To Fuck Marry Kill The American Way

3

Teen Spirit

They build walls
Draw lines
Force laws down throats
Broken treaties like missiles
Death childlike
Spilling blood on mothers faces

Military Haiku

war now forever white man bomb radiation into the future

Domestic Clocks and Brief Histories

(Darkness for 3 days x Abrus Precatorius)

Can't take no boat
Cant take the wind
Can't take my kin
Just these memories of how to escape
Guess we've done this before/begin

Equations For Dispersal

1

Delagoa Bay
Sotho-Tswana
Kholi
Nguni
Portuguese Maritime Expansion
Sharifian Dynasty
Cape Blanco

2

Susquehannock
Mohawk
Oneida
Cayuga
Seneca
Shawnee
Cherokee
Tuscarora

X+1 -> forward X + 2 -> Backward External Circle
(I can square that circle)

Evolutionary Thermodynamics
F (H x A) D C

-       *(R. Philips)*

Equation for Cruise-Ships

Trinidad
Cape Verde
Louisiana
Ghana
Infrastructure
Peru
Mexico
Black People
Hawaii
We
Caribbean
Rio
Lisbon
Imperialism
Nairobi
Barbados
Alabama
Finding/Searching Africa
We All Are
Finding/Searching Africa

Equation for Islands

We so Black
We think we
not the same

Equation For Down South

They can't afford to see you rise up
out of folklore
out from under
the guts of color ism
racism ism

Equation for Mayors (2021)

A Proximity To Death
In one year 3 thousand Black Women disappeared in Chicago

Equations 96 - 100

96

If there are no racists
Why are scientists building Slave ships?

97

Who is Gatson? (solve)
Who is William Wilberforce? (find value)

98

(Emancipation = Compensation) + 46,000 (Slave owners)
claims and counterclaims + propaganda wars = (solve) + 7

Answer (Britain)

99

A small little fishing village invests in a Slave voyage
(solve)

Answer (Liverpool Wins)

100

The many promises of freedom
In what year did African Americans acquire freedom in America?

a)   1964
b)   2045
c)   Never
d)   1875
e)   3033
f)   4022
g)   2016
h)   1870

Code Red Q

Is it code red or cold dead? (solve)

Death Equation

How many minutes?
How many warnings?
How much pressure?
How much ignorance?
How many Mothers?
How many Sons?
How many Daughters?
How many Femmes?
How many Trans?
How many Fathers?
How many are watching?
How many recordings?
Seville?
Canary islands?
Treaty of Tordesillas?
Pope Alexander?
Queen Isabella?

No windows in a box guess we dead
Guess it's over our head
Maybe we matter she said
Let me go ask master
I'll tell you what he said
The world's a ghetto
Just ask the bedbugs in my bed

(Solve for Liberation)

Hold It Near The Flame My Child

They Ask A Lot Questions
Fast Questions
Questions That Go Around In Circles
Questions That Trap You & Hold You Near The Fire
Push Your Face In The Flame
In Front Of The Judge
The Court
The 3 Headed Hydra
The Mouth Of An Empty Well

You've Got Me Inbetween The Devil And The Deep Blue Sea.
In The Still And The Chill Of The Night
Hell Froze Over
Retrocausality
The 3 Headed Realty
Right Head Eating America
Left Head Eating The Blues

Come Up Water Come On Up

The Universal Mother
The Time Machine
Felt Time Silk Stockings
Shiva Dancing to Prince
Ebony And Bronze
Sound And Thought Of Mind
Dreams And Ideologies
If you only knew how special you are

The Black Sun
Holy Science
If Only You Knew Like How Patti Labelle Sing

Come On Up Water Come Up

If you only knew

Equation for Finding Value

me
after
me
after
me
in the sweat of
me
before
negro
negroes
nega
nig
you
before
you
divided
you
In
to
Zero

We Are

Our sum has been beyond any understanding of the mathematics they stole from us

Boom Bap Time Equation

Greg Tate
The voice of a village
A New York minute
Hold it in your hand

Microphone Pen Paper Guitar
Hendrix Ritual Of Fire
See It Come Alive
See It Unfold And Reform
See It Turn Into A Dove
See It Fly Away
I wanna go outside in the rain
Didn't It Rain Purple Rain
Didn't It Rain Purple Rain
Got Our Rock & Roll Antennas Wet
Now We Official Intelligence
From One Funkadelic To Another
Hi Fi Liberation Technologies
Hard Bop Intelligence
Blue Black Magic Matrix Brother From Another Earth Seed
Planet Making With Words
Word Magi Brother With Dem Golden Hands
Scribe On Graffiti Walls Inside And Outside
Institutions Of Ghetto Archive

You Returned It All
Repo Man

Reclaimed
Made It Ours Eternal
Made Us A Space Station
Made Us A Home
Of Language
Of Truth
Of Loud Feedback
Flushing Rose Petals From Harlem Concrete To Uptown Bricks

Our Collective Sonic Hearts Beat
Brown Sugar Spills Out

Geometry for the Reversal of Whatisms, An Equation for the Afterlife
(for my Cousin Bev)

They gave her a month to live
she said i'll take that +2 (more) days
to take in the earth and air of my family
to be in the embrace of a root
the root of persistence

Erasing the temporality of they death clock

Clock Fight
(Lyric Equation)

Aint gotta fight no more
I done fought the kitchen clock
I done fought the masters clock
I done fought work clock
I done fought the god clock
I done fought the tax clock
I done fought the rich clock
I done fought the poor clock
I done fought the city clock
I done fought the country clock

I wish it was a fight it's more like a war, a thousand looping years of the same

Equation for Flight 0009

My Father went to Vietnam
Not on vacation
Not on vacation

Ghosts at our door dancing

Hide
Go seek
Hang
Go get
Hide
Go seek
Hang
Go get Out

The war
The woods
The plantations
The graveyards
The projects

Ghosts at yo door *Dancing*

Catwalk
Shotgun
Planking

Go in

Mbende Jerusarema
Indlamu
Ukusina
Lamba
Kpanlogo
Moribayassa
Zouglou
Kwassa Kwassa
Zaouli

Equations for Timekeepers
Religious x Clocks Christian Calendars

Tick Tock
Aggression/Suppression
Tick Tock
Tick Tock
Imperialism/Colonialism
Tick Tock
James River
London Virginia Company
Somers Isles Company
King James
Charles II
The Southern Department
British Crown
Board Of Trade And Plantations
Canada
Florida
Bahamas
War And Colonial Office
King Philip's War
The Molasses Act
New Guinea
Chalmette Refinery
Tick Tock
9 Million Tons
Cuba
Jamaica
Barbados Sugar time
11 Million
Nicholas Bayard

Columbia University
One Police Plaza
Rhinelanders Sugar House
Old Sugar House Prison
Tick Tock
Mississippi River
The Havemeyers
Madison Avenue and 38th Street
125,000 souls from Louisiana

Equation for society 1

If love is odd, x + 1 is divisible by x + god

Equation For Society 2

1 + 1	2 (time)
1 + 1 + 1	3 (religion)
1 + 1 + 1 + 1	2 x 2 (government)
1 + 1 + 1 + 1 +	5 (race)
1 + 1 + 1 + 1 + 1 + 1	2 x 3 (slave)

Equation For Your Heart Opening

Hold this chaos poem in ur lap raise it up to be everything your pain doesn't allow you to be

Equation For Celestial Bodies

Earth Mirror
A Rush of Fire and Water
Hiding Forrest Feelings
We are not the Waters Reflection
We are the warped gathering of cyclone anthologies
Below the calm tide of new

Equation For Stolen Artifacts In London

12th Dynasty Old Kingdom Kahun Papyri University College London
Sande Mask Gold of the Akan Solid Bronze Arm Ring removed from
the Body of the Matabele Mzilikazi Victoria & Alberts Museum

088

Confederates Day Same Day As Martin Luther King Jr Day
They got em real good at the courthouse
On the balcony
In the graveyard
At the Robert E Lee elementary
Over there in Jefferson County
They got em real good
On the flag of Texas
On the highway Equation

089

Ranger danger
Pig spill
Hot hand trooper
It wont make yo heart real
Mary God Ezekiel
It wont make yo sin disappear
Adam God Joseph

090

1 when God = +2 (alpha) vs (government)
5 when God = +4 (adam) vs (nature)
12 when God = +3 (atom) vs (war)

091

Look out beyond read sky quilts listen to the water drums
Beware
Traps At the Head of South River
On the East side of Piccowaxen Creek
On Elk River
On the East Side of the Chesapeake Bay
Between the Heads of South and Severn Rivers

1

Rio Real
Santo Amaro
Camamu
Cairu
(**solve**)

2

Surinam
French Guiana
Djuka
Saramaka
Aluku
Paramaka
Kwinti
(**solve**)

3

1650
Hundred Thousand
Acapulco
Veracruz
Panuco
Valley of Mexico
(**solve**)

4

St. Anne
St. Elizabeth
Westmorland
St. James
Trelawney Town
Crawford Town
Nanny Town
(**solve**)

8 Towards A Present Infinity

8 cards

The Wheel Of Fortune
The World
The Sun
King Of Swords
The Fool
Queen Of Wands
Three Of Cups
The Hermit

8 Lines

Fate Line
Life Line
The Line Of Mercury
Simian Line
Line Of The Head
The Heart Line
The Line Of Apollo
Line Of Affections

8 Roots

Rattlesnake Root
Blood Root
Adam And Eve Root
Ginger Root
Turmeric Root
Garlic Root
Dandelion Root
Burdock Root

24 Portals

Cauldron

8 Hearts (Watching Over Me)

ELLA MAE
URSULA
JAMAR
HANK
GARY
EDWIN
BEVERLY
JONES LOR J

8 Parts *(Formula Number 3)*

Copper 100%
Platinum 100%
Pure Gold
Alkaline Water
Soma Plant Juice
Silver
Black Resin
Flux

8 Lessons (Naqshbandi)

Recollection
Awareness of Breathing
Pause of the Heart
Pause of Time
Pause of Numbers
Solitude in Company
Remembering
Restraint

Eternity Is A Life Act Of Infinite Intensity

By and by for my Grandmother
A trio of Ella's
So I feel a root
A god hymn
A spell thing

Deep Philadelphia Roots
Deep Maryland Roots
Deep Chesapeake Roots

Equations for Sisters at Church

Oooooh I'm telling
I'm telling mama
I saw you kissing
Oooooh I'm telling
soon as we get home
I'm telling

you was right there
I saw you in church
under Jesus
kissing
and Jesus was looking
just a looking at you

Did Jesus say anything?
What did Jesus say?

Family Equation
(made a circle)

yo Mommas Baby
yo Momma Momma
yo Sista
yo Auntie Sister
yo Grandma
yo Great Great Grand
yo Nanas Sister
made a circle
with
sage
gold
ash
& water

She said, put all the bad shit away Momma made a circle that'll keep
us all safe

Architecture 1

I found a room to pray
See a prayer needs room
A direct body
A portal Of temporal agency

Come on in the room
Circle of ash we are protected
The oils burn & sweat essence of self
Multitudes
Celestial
Pathways of becoming
What we are/be/was already
Particle
Image
Imagi

Architecture 2

Its so cheap its face
Trying to recount
The reason
The earth wind and fire
The reasons we are here
Only The Dust, The Ash, The Blues know
Deep in the Juke joint forest of our Granny's land
Land over
Land done turnt us over
We grown
Over run wild greens
Deep magenta Roots magi
Eyes swirled malachite
Trying to re collect

Architecture 3

We drove right past
Nelson Coleman Correctional Center

And didn't even see the fire at
St. John the Baptist Parish it was 7 o'clock at
Marmillion's plantation the bell rung
The German Coast uprising 1811
Nat Turner
Angola's cane
Knights of Labor,
1752 to 1975
New River plantation
Stapleton estate
Colonial exhibit at the world's fair
Christ Church Nichola Town
The Bore Slave Labor Camp
The Lives Of Living Death

Architecture 4

Brother Marvin I hear you cry when you sing to us
Beautiful warnings of what's coming
Oh the weight of what's to come
No Nation
No Ownership
No Foundations of Stability
In the Red
Education Flat Line
Poverty Tent City Line
I've been away for a long time
Long gone outa heart and mind
Can you tell me what's happening brother
What's been going on?
Break my heart slowly

I look into the feelings of the people
The eyes of the people
The rhythm of the people
Break my heart slowly brother

Long Time No Past

Rocket Ship Rocket
Destination Unknown
What Planet is this?
Baby All We Got Is Stardust From Tomorrow
In The Orbit Of Ra
A Black Mass
Light Hours Felt Empty
Baraka Bible Of Truth
The Oracle Of Dumas
Don't Worry
I Stole Time Just To Be here with you
i don't have all the answers
I been sending letters back home to mothers of invention
Letters Full of truth questions

Was It Ever So Simple
Death Feels Haunting
 Like Gza Shadow Boxing New Methods Of Being
Is Change Ever Coming
Obama Portals Of New Deals And Promise
Operation Brutality
Great Depression Shock And Awe
Dear Mama
Help!

I will bring up the dead to eat the living
- A note from the poet

Harmonic Endings 1 & 2
(Voodoo the evil back into the great white spook)

Friday We Heard About A War
World War Three
We Pulled Out Our Nuclear Arms
Hugged Each Other Not Waiting To Let Go
Saturday A Rocket Hit Inside The Green Zone
5,000 American Troops Already In Iraq
60,000 In The Region
14,000 Added Since May
3,000 American Troops To Kuwait
The 82nd Airborne Division's 1st Brigade Combat
Uss Harry S. Truman Is Currently
In The Gulf Of Oman With Hundreds Of Tomahawk Cruise Missiles
Still Looking For Weapons Of Mass Destruction
Still Wiping Away The Trail Of Tears
Still Without Heart Eyes Humanity
Still Death Agents
Still Rabid Still Bleeding From The Eyes Still Reptilian
Still Generals Of Genocide
A Prayer For Us Lost In War
Fugitives And Neighbors
Children Screaming For Justice
Mothers Throwing Fire Bombs
Fathers Crying Tears Of Abuse

2

Before we let go
before we become intoxicated in prayer
let us state the facts
humanity is a dead fish
deep fried
wrapped in today's
burning forest headline
just like our life
dead or full of plastic

MUSIC INDUSTRY EQUATIONS 1

What was the value of Elvis in morally bankrupt America?

MUSIC INDUSTRY EQUATIONS 2

How much money does Paul MaCartney owe Little Richard?
How much money do the Rolling Stones owe Little Richard?
How much money does Jerry Lee Lewis owe Little Richard?
How much money does Buddy Holly owe Little Richard?
How much money do the Everly Brothers owe Little Richard?

MUSIC INDUSTRY EQUATIONS 3

How much did Leadbelly get paid driving Lomax around to get them interviews?

American Equations In Black Electronic Music

In Search of Liberation Technologies
Arp Fantasies
Keyboard fantasies
Gospel Organ truths
Free Jazz Dreams of a better life
Modular briefcase
One way ticket
To pitchfork insurrections

MUSIC INDUSTRY EQUATIONS 4

How many Blues musicians were killed by Columbia, Chess, Atlantic, Specialty Victor, Vocalion, and Paramount Records?

MUSIC INDUSTRY EQUATIONS 5

Founders Fund
Goldman Sachs
2 billion US Dollars
Back office handshakes
Deals with the devil
Don't say Chess Records 3x times in the mirror
Read the warning label
Send the fine print to NASA

MUSIC INDUSTRY EQUATIONS 6

How much money do the Rolling Stones owe Tina Turner?
How much money do the Rolling Stones owe Bo Diddley
How much money do the Rolling Stones owe Chuck Berry?
How much money do the Rolling Stones owe Bobby Womack?
How much money do the Rolling Stones owe Willie Dixon?
How much money do the Rolling Stones owe Robert Johnson?

BLUES TIME

Black Legacies Universal Equations And African Sonic Traditions

Harmonic 7th Blues 7 minor 7th 0070788398020404202477777
Blues Scales The Blues Foundation 0203090659705090400009
Parallels in Tone, Color, and History 707077207027407270270
Red Tones and Black Symphony 87878375300728738748070
Between Minutes and Melodies 767836763222297890000000
Blues Time Reimagined Unraveling the Clock temporal Grooves
Clocks and Blues The Future of Blues Time Syncopated Hours
Blues Time in the Rhythm 093099023973479000209307862
The Blues Time Continuum We came back for you.
Long grain rice water. Up to our waist

Once Upon A Time
(Elvis Went To Jail)

George W. Johnson
The Laughing Song
Dandy Darky
Let's take a long look in
The mirror called America
Let's dance around the beginning and end

Let's laugh Yesterday's pain away

> *Ha ha ha ha ha,*
> *Woo ha ha ha ha ha ha ha ha,*
> *Woo ha ha ha ha ha ha ha ha,*
> *Ha ha ha ha ha ha ha ha ha,*
> *Ha ha ha*

Them Texas Jails
Hang Time
Dead Time
Death Clock

Long Walk
Hand And Hand With The Bush And His Senior

Towards The Dark Light
The Black Hole
The American Flag

They Stole My Hound Dog
My Muddy Water
My Beer
My Home
My Junk Joint
My Blacknuss
My Reeds And Deeds
My Gifts & Messages
My Bright Moments

My Electric Mud
My Wang Dang Doodle
My Ball n' Chain
My Diamond Teeth
My 3 Sided Dream

They Stole Our Sound
And Tried To Sell Us
They Southern Cross
They Pig
They Flag
They Country Twang
They Honky Tonk

FOLK TWANG BLUES
We Don't Play No Damn Rock N Roll & We Don't Play That Jazzy
Snazzy Shit

Music Business Is Gridiron Business

It's Just Lies And Dreams
Hit After Hit
Brainstorming Ideas
Minds Rockefeller To American Dream States
On Bended Knee

This Is A Dream World Of Pain
We All Live Here
Pig Iron Blood Prayers
On Bended Knee

Married
Cloud Judgements
Lonely Delusions
Sideshow Hurt Misdirected Pain
Zeus Lightning Folding Events Together Forever
Pain Pretending To Comfort

In The End
Dear Lord
In The Wind
Dear Lord
I Hope To Know
A Body Again
Self Regenerating

Blues As Religion

I need me a prescription
A prescription for the Blues
Blues explosion
Shooting star Blues
Sundown Blues
Blues as religion

12 Bar Blues when i think about myself
Blues Scales of weightlessness
Blue Notes of love to one's self
A Blues Walk inside the language of love
A Blues Shuffle back to ourselves
16 Bar Blues in Spirit
I got the Spirit
Rain down Blues
We wet in god's tears

Spook and holler
Blues as religion
Sundown Blues
Shooting star Blues
Blues explosion
I need a prescription for the Blues
Spook and holler
Blackness as religion.
Sundown Blackness
Shooting star Blackness
Black explosion

The Blues & Me
Healing

BLUES TIME I

It Is Up To Us
It Has Always Been
The Griot Of The Sea
The Blue Truth Of Sky
Ma Rainey's Black Bottom Of Sound & Fire
The Moon Moanin
It's Blues Time
A Waltz For Beverly
Giant Steps A Return To Forever
Destination Out Heavy Weather
The Sidewinder From Winyah Bay to Kongo River
It's Blues Time Ella Shepard & John Westley Work Jr
The Tuskegee Quartet in Hampton Virginia
Marian Anderson & Paul Robeson singing Ezekiel Saw The Wheel In
West Africa
Sonny Sitt from Saginaw Michigan Saying It's Blues Time
No Body Knows The Trouble I've Seen
Pentecostal It was the BLOOD
Night Train New Orleans
Rock My Soul In The Bosom Of Abraham
It's Blues Time Oh Freedom
Eye On The Prize
Fisk Jubilee
Mamie Smith
Zora Neale Hurston
My Lord Is Writing Down Time
Every Day Will Be Sunday, Bye And Bye
Blessed Assurance
Ishmon Bracey
Willie Brown & Geeshie Wiley
The Darlings of Rhythm
Rosa Lee Hill
The Back Door Wolf in Clay County Mississippi
It's Blues Time
Roll over Beethoven
Tidal Wave
Highwater Everywhere

Blind Lemon Jefferson
How Long How Long Blues
Lord It's One Kind Favor I'll Ask Of You- See That My Grave Is Kept Clean

Dear Lord & Cotton Kingdom

I Was African In New Orleans
Old Corn Meal & Gumbo Ya-Ya
I Was Black In New York
Cotton Club Parades
The Lords Of Slavery
God's Trombone
Drums And Shadows
I Was A Sharecropper In Charleston
Sketches In Color
Mississippi Narratives & Sinful Tunes
The Big Payback
8, 9, 10, Ready Or Not Here I Come
Deep River Heaven
Sea Island Sweetgrass
Consciousness Correspondence
Our Meeting In The Woods
Long Mournful holler Swaying Swinging Down To Touch The Dirt
When The Day Begin To Crack The Bell Rang Blues
17th Century Harmonies
The Unusual Task Of Being Black in Blues
Been In The Storm So Long
I Don't Remember Where I Put My Guitar Let Alone My Strength
But Gods Will Gon Get Me Through
Deep Skin Fire In My Bones
Whip Hoe And Sword Revolt
The Religious Life Of Me Becoming
Under The Oak Tree
Under The Palmetto
Ritual Work Songs And Ballads
Ring Shout Traditions And Testimonies
The Secret Eye Watching

So We Pass It Down
Quilting New Language
Because When They Gone They Gone
Big Holes In The Quilts
Repetitions That Promised To Be Endless

See They Will Never Understand
The Communal Aspect Of The Blues
The Call And Response
The Give And Take
The Exchange
The I Owe You Back
The Low Hum
The Turning The World Upside Down
Shaking Its Foundation
Disrupting Heaven And Hell
Free From Work
Free From Death
Free From Everything
Free From The Bells
Bells In The Morning
Bells Around Necks
Bells Around The Hounds Trained To Hunt Down A Dream Escaping
Free From The Sounds
The Cries
The Selling And Buying
Families Torn Apart

See I Want My Own Sounds
My Own Kind Of Silence
My Own Time To Listen To The Morning Light Moan About Love

BLUES TIME II

Holy Of Holies
Sun Moon Fire Prayer
Creatures Of Darkness And Mythical Powers
Earth Mother Water Speak To Me

We Tried Everything To Get Heaven And Earth Together
Ask Zachariah
We Broke The Powers Of Nature
Air Fire Water Conspiracies Against Earth
We Had Iron Conversations
Thunder Stones
My Lord Of Darkness And Night
We Tried Everything

We Need Jade
Born In The Womb Of Earth
An Embryonic Stone
Turns Out There's 9 Heavens
Don't Know Which Heaven We Was Trying To Reach
All We Had Was a Compass Trying To Climb The Mountain Of
The Sun

Now That's The Blues
Movement And Sound Dissolved Into The Color Of Dreams
See That's The Blues Day Following Night
Midnight Blue Translucent In The Natural World
Walking Down That Road To Infinity
Sometimes The Blues Is Not Of This World
It Is Transcendent Wisdom
The Heart Of Pharaoh
Chaos At The Beginning Of Time
Midnight Water
Voyage To Atlantis
Midnight Hues
Voyage To The Sea Islands
Dark Noon
A Window To The Universe

The Reason WHY THE PREACHER DRESSES IN BLACK
The Spiritual Sun the Image Of Eternity
Solar Revelation
Soul Revolution
The Invisible Power
Animus
African Spiral Songs
African Spiral Dances
Moving In The Midst Of Things
That's The Blues
Ring Shouts
The Golden Flower
The Double Projection
Shadow Of Enlightenment
Among The Voodoos Black Magic Folk Remedies
The People's Medicine

I Caught A Flash Of The Spirit
Listening to J. T "Funny Papa" Smith
Seven Sisters Blues
Sundown Blues
The Blues Time Travelers
Robert Johnson
Clara Smith
Rahsaan Roland Kirk
Aunt Caroline Dye
Bessie Brown
Louisiana Hoodoo Blues
Lizzie Miles
Black Herman Rucker
Oku Aba
Listening to Muddy Waters
It Felt Like The Discovery Of The Future

Long Live The Earthshaker Koko Taylor
Chesapeake Bay Catfish Blues
Dust My Broom I'm Going Back To Ethiopia
Listening to Howlin Wolf
Tampa Red Jazz Me Blues and Make Me Nice
The Count Basie Orchestra
One O'clock Time Jump
Portal Time
QuantaFro

BLUES TIME III

The Cosmos As A Vibration
Let Us Return To The Gospel
A Spiritual Of Many Dimensions
A Total Lunar Eclipse
Shadow Frequencies
From Myth To Mathematics
From Myth To Physics
The Last Transit Of Venus
Let Us Return To The Gospel
Inverted Rainbows Dancing Patterns Of Nature
Sublime Visions Fractal Illuminations
Gospel laborers
We Prayed And Prayed And Prayed Again
It's Quitting Time

We Learned Some Truths
Beyond The River
Forbidden Fruits And Lessons
When We Feel Dead
Awaken
Rise Up
Sound Out To Our Legends
Ntozake Shange *
Sonia Sanchez
Geri Allen
bell hooks
Octavia Butler
Audre Lorde

We Found Family
Daughters Of Thunder
Fourteen Hundred Cowries
Magic Drums From Dahomey
This Dark Cloud Won't Hold Me
Sun Going Down
Hearing Is Seeing
And Now We Know
Why The Jaybird Goes To See The Bad Man On Friday

BLUES TIME IV

The Chemistry Of Color
An Acoustic Event
Seeing Darkness At Night
Protect Your Secrets From Human Perception
The Theory Of Ideas

We Work
We Live The Work
Golden Gate Quartet
Jook Joints & Barrel Houses
Root Doctors
Obeah
Odu
Banganga
Mamoni Lines
We Have A Continual Beginning
Sacred Geometry

In The Midst Of Or The Aftermath Of
Black Codes
Black Laws
Code Noir
North Carolina Slave Courts
Piedmont Virginia
Tacky's Revolt
The Pope In Britain
Slave Codes
Slave Patrols
Barbados Slave Codes
The House Of Burgesses
Ancient Roman Codes & Traditions
Laws Of The Indies
South Carolina Slave Codes
The Virginia Slave Codes Of 1705
Ohio Black Codes
All Locked Away
The History Of The Devil
Mind/ Body Snatchers

BLUES TIME V

They Turned Their Backs On The World

The Science Of Remembering Everything
Folk Tales Of Nighttime
Stories Of Midnight Blues & Mapping The Moon
Stories Of Working The Spirit

See You Got To Work The Spirit In You
Call Out On Front Street
Get Electrified
Speak Tongues
Work Up A Sweat

Smash The Virtual Window
Understand The Lies Of Democracy
The Way Injustice Laughs In Yo Face After Calling You Ugly
The Unraveling Western Mind
American Psycho

The Watching
High Ivory Towers
Underground Tunnels
Drones From Cambridge

The Nra Returning To The Plantation
The Past & Future As Revelations
Returning To Factories Of Mind
Or Like Lonnie Holley Say
Industrial Fields

We Know Secret Origins
Between Knowing And Calling Ourselves Back
4th Dimensional Telescopes
The Virgin As Hourglass Feeling Time Pass
The Red Dress As The Crystal Sun
We Must Remember To Rest
Because Somehow The King Is Still Horny
Disenchanted Splendor

Sacrificing History For Now Pleasures
Present Day Distractions
A Love Affair With The Filtered Image
Ceremonies Of Disconnect

When Roots Die
When Our Roots Die

No Religious Movements
No Ritual Structures
No Art Of Conjuring
No Sorcery
No Downhome Blues
No Root Doctor
No Low Down Mojo Blues
No Prophecies
No Spirit Possession
No Hoodoo
No God Struck Me Dead And Brought Me Back To Life
No Folklore
No Two Headed Doctors
No Ray Charles
No Sonny Terry
No Chuck Berry
No Little Richard
No Ira Tucker
No Bo Diddley
No Zora Neale Hurston
No Albertina Walker
No Fats Domino
No John Lee Hooker
No Dorothy Norwood
No Roberta Martin
No Della Reese
No Mahalia Jackson
No Sister Rosetta Tharpe
No Clara Ward
No Aretha Franklin
No Dorothy Love Coates
No Claude Jeter

InfiniRoot - Black Quantum

Spatial Ambiguity
Who Owns Our Truths
The Mirror In Time
Industrialization Of Light Reflecting
Free Love And Spacetime

17,400 Kilograms Of Clocks
Bell Tower Crashing Down On Our Heads
Fear Knots!

We Are The Temporal Deprogrammers
In The Battle Of Clock & Bible
We Are Ready
Templex Think Tank
See I Got The Word In Me And I Can Say It
Teleporting An Unknown Boko
Quantum Vodun

We Have Reached The Nubianexus
False Time And True Time
Third & Fourth World Time
9th ward time
Grandmother Time
Space Time
Interdimensional Time
Mirror Time
Colored People's Time
MOTHER TIME
Universal Time
Non Local Time
Daylight Saving Time
Colonial Times
Africa unite time
BQF TIME
Black Studies Time
Clock Time

War Time
God Time

Can These Bones Live?
Can These Spirits Time Bend?
Do These Ghosts Know Master Juba?
Something Faster Than The Speed Of Light

Our Love Entangled
We Knew
You Dreamed
I Balanced
We Climbed
Swam Back Out
Pass The Rice Fields
Pass The Ankh
Up To Hilton Head Island

We Made A Quantum Event Map
Then Headed Down To Savannah
River Walk
Headhunters
Holographic Ghosts
X Dimensions
White Darkness
White Holes
The Cemeteries Of Academia
Gravitational Collapse
Where Is History Going?
Out Of Order Chaos
The Quantum Leap
Veritempo

Human Robotic Invention
The Black Matrix Speaks To A Time
Maybe A Present But Not A Future
Maybe More Of A Hope But Not A Multitude

Vulnerability
Pitless Wisdom
The Sentence Could Dance Circles
Re-Order The Logic Of Science Fiction

A Formula
A Complexity
Tempoal Landscapes
Womanist Temporal- Scapes Breaking Down Time
By Virtue Of Being A African Woman
Annie Turnbo Malone

AfroQuark

Temporal Deprogramming
Radical Imagination
A Hazzard County Called The Past/Future
No Machines Exist
She Breaks The Paradox

Shook Physics

I Found Some Spells
Castor Oil
Cunjuh
Lavender Oil
Gin
Sugar
Clove
Dried Orris Root
Sage

Yang Blues Particles

Fats Navarro Etta James Soundwave
Hugh Masekela Mariam Mekeba Sonorous
Yusef Lateef Alice Coltrane Sonare
Billy Higgins Abbey Lincoln Resound
Philly Joe Jones Maya Angelou Sounding
Billy Cobham Alice Walker Re-Sound
Al Jarreau Amiri Baraka Sonogram
Johnny Hartman Lucile Clifton Sonant
Wes Montgomery Phyllis Hyman Sonus
Stanley Clarke June Tyson Soundness
Lee Morgan Jayne Cortez Soundboard
Cootie Williams Moor Mother Re-Echo

GOSPEL TEXAS USA
New Minority Blame Poverty Blame Memory

Hold Me In The River
Sweet Home Baptist Church
Take Me Down To River
To A Deeper Past
Before The Oil
Before The Master Plan
Before The Masters Clock

We Can All Be Free Here
We Been Here Before Them
This Is Ours

This Belongs to Us
Forever entangled in History
Ghosts Of Memory

I Remember

How Amazing It Was
To Be A Part Of Something
A Communal Song
A Folk Rhythm
A Glorious Echo
Stretching Out
Never Ending

I Remember

The Knowing
The Founding
The Freeing
The Fleeing
The Nourishment
Of Home

Never Late Prelude

Jazz In The Red
For Profit For Sale
Sold
Going Out Of Business
In Debt
Deported
Evicted
Absorbed
Kicked Out Unhoused
Brought Out Pushed Out
Gone Missing Destroyed
Lynched Murdered
Hunted
Trapped Beheaded
Non Hue No Pulse No Breath

Jazz In The Black
No'Clock Service
Master of Ceremonies - Henry Giles
Opening Hymn - Ella Legarr
Short Talk - Issac Cole
Prayer - Rachael Giles
Solo - Hurry Burn that Ship *by Julia Ann Blake*
Scripture Lesson - John Myers
Song - We Built this Country Lord and They Know It *by Wetipquin*
Baptist Choir
Scripture - Adela Durbin
Prayer - Melvina Lisby
Selection - Choir, Director Ernest Lisby
Sermon - Joseph Lisby
Song - No Time No Master *by Havre De Grace A.M.E Choir*
Hymn - We Know God *by Ella Myers & Joseph Broadway*
Sermon - Rev. Julia Cole
Offering - Phoebe Giles & Elizabeth Bishop
Doxology - Minnie Anderson & Henry Turner
BENEDICTION - Clara Broadway
Selection - I don't Trust Nobody *by Nathaniel Durbin & Cassandra Bond*

Blues For Scorpio

storm came twice today in honor of my mother i am born again
(water sky x universal womb x 9 month durational)

Blues For My Cousin Jamar

today is your birthday gone too soon future christ
(while you are sleeping x breathe waves)

Blues for Grandfathers

Eye Am Eye's Memory Alone
We Was Before
I Know
I Seent It
We Are Before/After/ Future Waves
Vibrations/ Holograms/Light
Sonic/ Color Omega/Genesis

Haiku Blues For Dorothy Ashby

soft winds sunflower detroit hip harp reflections theater griot

Haiku Blues For Melba Liston

Her bones volcano blues legacy ghostwriter color Jamaica

Haiku Blues For Geri Allen

sound detroit prayers sonic aspects of water the life of a song

Haiku Blues For Nancy Wilson

yesterday's blues now her voice coated in honey sweet cocoanut grove

Haiku Blues For Jayne Cortez

heart left a message a dance and cry for lovers words like wind like change

Haiku Blues For Carmen McRae

Live at sugar hill spirituals and holy ghosts carmen sings blue monk

This Planet Is A Scene Of A Crime

A practice of temporal deprogramming

1

Somehow it's over heads
And not quite towards a simple truth
Ok well here it goes

Eyes of danger
Misspoken words
Wrong translations
Odd volumes & Odd times
Will leave u dead

Drive by highway kingdom come
A million caskets in the river
Its tar river
Cancer alley
It's George Bush
Bill Clinton
Its stolen land and bloodhounds

Death patrol since 1739
In wilmington
1751 in philadelphia
Nothing special
Broken timelines
We know a mob is a mob
Demented senile rabid
foaming at the mouth psychotic
Robotic state of mind

See the whole estate was for sale
And we aint know it
Now we dance and sing

Inside the thing
While the thing controls the thing we invented
Inverted life sentence

2

How to unwork the line
On the line
Opening up to quantum thought
released from it specialism
Open up to all SPACE - TIMES
Think black and quantum
Retrocurrents
Retrocausality

Seeing the future
Mental models
Seeing the future
Not necessarily in front of us but beyond

Temporal deprogramming From seconds to centuries

Time Signals
Time Quilts
Time Equations
Time Paradox
Time Scales

I heard you singing
Deep in the jook
Singing something like
Time changes & floods right on in
Blues Time and Temporal Alchemy

Q Futurism

The Sun of a Black Unknown
Ghost Black Blue Spectrum & Oya
Daughter of a Planet called Tanzania
The one who causes the throat to breathe
Who lives in the Blood Milk of our Quantum Mothers

If you know a woman, you know a thing under the water
-             Temme proverb

Water Rag

Water me
Water me revolution
The water teaches
Internal energy spirit essence
Love & revelation
Baptism by water
By blood
By desire
Of earth
Of salt
Of ash
Her ghost with fire

She/They
Who shows us the way to the stars
The shiting image
Escape/Exit/Reorder/Reimagine
Pathways cosmic no - time order
Kosmos Of the world
Worldly
World order
Earthly
The world of people
To prepare
To adorn
The universe

We Map these Realities / Moments of the Sun

Queen-of-Kongo
Ki-Kongo
Mbanza Kongo
Kongo Cosmogram
Yowa
Nzambi Mpungu
Ntoto
Mpemba
Kalunga
Lunga
Mpati
Mpati
Power
Power

We Meditate To Pass Through The Emotiportal/Senseship

Go Into The Dark And Pull Out The Night
Pull It Out Blinding
White Rainbows Of Desire
Desires To Be On Fire
Dim Lit Stars
Light Hours Burning

How Long Has It Been?
Light Minutes?
Light Hours?
Since We Seen Any Life Lines

The Roots From Which Creation Is Born
Water/Fire
Wood/Metal/Earth
Phases of Harmony
Know Whiteness
Maintain Blackness
Firmament

Quantum Black In The Moment

I Danced Through The Trials Of My Father
A War Dance
Umzansi
A Child Alone In The World
Back Against The Tree Of Family
Strong Winds Of Gratitude
Collecting Seeds Growing Future Fathers
Outside Of Drug & Prisons Wars
American Encores Of Injustice

(Is Sound A Quantum Event?)
- Black Quantum Futurism

Quantum
Black
In The Moment
Stacked Up Particles
Reverend Leon Sullivan
Aero Space Agency
North Philly Satellite
Dox Thrash Painting Shadows Of The Future
Ridge Ave Gateway
Free Jazz Highway
Low Groan Bubbling
Coltrane Strawberry Mansion A Love Supreme
Plasma Through Concrete
The Persistent Past
High Screeching
Feedback Sister Rosetta
Looping The Ever Present Wave
Quantum Black In The Moment

The Black Time Belt & Its Quantum Future

From Can't See To Can't See - Let Us Acknowledge The Sun.
We Are Living In The Alchemy Of Our Ancestors' Futures.
We Are The Quantum Result Of The Beautiful Madness (Kosmic Kaos)

Quantum Sun

I Was Never Here Just A Continuous Echo In A Strange Land

I Was A Quantum Event

On This Planet

Desolate & Dangerous

The Devil's Playground

The Deviled Egg Without A Moon

I Was The Blinking Particle

In & Out Of Orbits

And On Earth I Ain't Heard

No Cosmic Tones
No Afrofuturism
So Please Keep Me Out Your Make Believe Futurisms
And Don't Put Me On Any Timelines
Because From 1619 To Wakanda I Don't Exist

Whose Math Is This?
Whose Timeline?
Who's Black Is This?
Who's Master's Clock?
Who's Whip Beat Through Eternity?
Who's Journey?

Ain't No Humanity On Earth
That's Why We Travel The Space-Ways
See It Ain't No End
The Music They Making On Earth
Lullabies For The Devil
PUT YOU TO SLEEP IN A TRANCE DAZED OUT
DUMBFOUNDED BEAT BY BEAT

You Better Get Back On That Mother Ship Punch In Your Cosmic
Time Slip And Be Gone Be Born A New A Network Organic Matter
Quantum Mildew The Music That Talks To The Trees Tells Them
To Breathe Music That Can Be Both Satellite And Transmission

A Landing Station For Intergalactic Space Travel

Thomas Stanley Said Our Strength Is The Truth Of Time
So Let Me Say It

These Times Aint True
These Choking Times
The Air Is Leaving
Our Brother The Wind Is Leaving
Our Ocean Mother Is Leaving
Time Flies With The Tide
Time Flies In The Courthouse
Ain't That The Truth

            Well Don't Be No Truth In The Eyes Of The Vultures
            Don't Be Truth In Carnegie Hall
            Don't Be Truth After It's All Been Bought And Paid For
            Don't Be Truth Looking Into The Sonic Mirror It May
            Recognize You
            And Pull You In
            Space Time Continuum

            Was This Just Supposed To Be Nice?

            Nighttime Suns

Darkness Skies
No Blue Without The Sun
No Blues Without The Sun
Without The Sun There Is No Day Dreaming
When I'm Thinking Of You
There Is No Day Dreaming
When I'm Thinking Of You
There Is No Day
Only Tomorrow

Will I See You Tomorrow
On That Strange Cosmic Road
Will I See You Tomorrow
Improvising With Shango
On The Other Side Of The Sun

Who Will Survive America
Who Will Survive The Cosmos

A Black Quantum Futurism
A Theory & Practice
Of No Time
Of No Temporal Alliance

The Black Time Belt Stretches
Its Hands Beyond The Reach Of Gods
The Black Galactic Space Station Is Gold
A Dessert On Fire
Brass Drums
The Other Side Of The Sun
The Invisible Shield
A Universe In Blue

Next Time You Go Out Just Listen
Free Jazz Improvised Liberation Tech - No Music
It Is The Only Gateway For Humanity To See In To The
Unknown

They Are Mining Our Futures

Bags Of Bones Tossed Out In To The Cosmos
Let's See Where They Land Float

Read The Bones
Read The Bones

What Do They Say, New York?
Read The Bones
Read The Bones

What Do They Say, Saturn?

Read The Bones
Read The Bones

What Do They Say, Atlantis?

Read The Bones
Read The Bones

What Do They Say, Chicago?
Read The Bones

No Notes To Transcribe This To Another Language

Read The Bones
Feel Yourself Knowing
Hear The Sound
Listen

The Ark Is Leaving Brothers - Sisters - Theys & Thems

The Ark Is Leaving For The Only Place That Understands Gravity
Africa
Meet Me In Nubia

Building Galactic Sound Sculptures

Meet Me In The Quantum Archives
We Must Be Leaving
They Are Mining Our Past
The Sun's Planet

Who Gonna Pay For The Memories?
They Lock Up The Memories
Make Us Pay
Turn Us Out

Junkie Nostalgia
Find Yourself At The Met With A Bomb Demanding Back Ur Memories

But The Truth Is Your Memories Been Gone / Be Gan /
Be Kin/ Bee Hive
A Photograph With No Ink No Eye No Sun
Lo Hums Lo Ohms Hi Hertz Hi Freq

You Already Been Bought And Sold
You Can't Sell What You Don't Own

See They Brought Me In Here In To Recalibrate The Frequencies
At The Heart Of This Place Is A Sonic Mirror
Humans Are Instruments
And At Some Point
We Must Come To Terms With Our Reflection In This Sonic Mirror

It's All Cheap
All This Music
All This Traveling
And Where Have We Been
Stuck On An Advertisement
No Movement No Rhythm No Heart
Just Add Water Just-Add Color
Just Add Sound

You Just Packaged Dust
And We Gotta Pretend That You Understand Music
Well Everything And Everyone Is Music
But You Gotta Be Real Quiet To Hear It
And You Can't Be On Sale Or Sold Out

The Voice Of The Eternal Tomorrow Is Calling Us Home
We Never Learning To Listen
We Never Learning To Listen To The True Source
We Can Not Hear
The Ending Is Your Desire
Save Us From Our Desires
Same Me From You

For I Am Not Like You

Currency For The Next Millennium
Moving Pictures
Imported Sounds
Imported Voices
Imported Feelings
Fake Sounds
Stock Instruments

Same Movie Same Themes
All Screaming The Same Empty Truth
A Truth That Never Did Us Any Good On This Planet

Land Of Odds At Odds With Itself
The Odds Are Choreographed Endings
Mostly Nightmares

Humanity Tugging On The Cloth Of Jee-Yus
Please Bring The Devil
Lost In The Dark Ages Of Man

Humanity An Organic Oil Spill Quantum Poison

Meet Me In Nubia
Building Galactic Sound Sculptures
Meet Me In The Quantum Archives

We Must Leave Be Leaving
They Are Mining Our Past

Plastic Sound Waves
Everything Left Is A Lie
Everything Sounding Beyond This Moment Is A Lie
Let Then Hear What The Trumpets Sound Like
And Any Other Sound Is A Lie

God Is More Than Love
Humans Don't Mix Love With God
They Don't Even Mix God With God
They Mix God With The Devil

Humanity Tugging On The Cloth Of Jee-Yus
Screaming Please Bring In The Devil
Lost In The Dark Ages Of Man
They Sing Please Bring In The Devil

They Are Mining Our Futures
Everyone Left Is A Lie
Everything Left Is A Lie
Fast Futures - Fast Lies -

Bio Degradation

Bags Of Bones Tossed Out In To The Cosmos
Let's See Where They Land Float

Read The Bones
Read The Bones

What Do They Say, Atlantis?

Read The Bones
Read The Bones
Read The Bones
Read The Bones

What Do They Say, Explorers?
What Do They Say, Artists?

No Notes To Transcribe This To Another Language
No Land To Map
This Is Another Dimension
So Below So Be Nigh
So Above So Abate
The Gravity Of Jazz True Suns

No Blue
No Blues
No Daydreaming
No Day
Only Tomorrow

Will I See You Tomorrow
Improvising With Oya On The Other Side Of The Sun
Surviving America
Surviving The Cosmos

A Black Quantum Future
No Time
No Temporal Alliance

The Reach Of Gods
The Black Galactic
Rhythm On Fire
Copper Drums
The Invisible Shield
The Universe In Gold

Light x Bends/Ends

Must Have Been An Explosion Of Orbits Trying To Deliver The Truth But Got Caught Up In The Beauty Of itself.

Sit down Let me lend you a word
Something for when things get heavy
Something stronger than no
First go tell them i'm here
In memory
A circuit
In the familiar
A meridian
A blues people
Tell them im here—let them see me
I Made my way through the digital underground
Sampling past present future me
I get around—in the world of mind
Downstairs Blues Uptown
See—this—is—what it is Time flashing its lights
Pulling the plug
While you still performing
See this is what it is
You Got To Be The Love—You Been Waiting For
You Gotta Listen—And Know
How Important You Are
Your Sound Essence
Your Ritual Towards Freedom
Our Work Unseen But Felt
Don't Be Lost In The Shadows
Look In The Shadows
No Longer Trapped in the dark
My people look within
Find the light I'm right by the light
The light got a hold of me
I can't stop shining
We might be the Sun
We might be the Sun

Blues Legacies Universal Equations

It may strike a verve
Make you bleed blue blood notes
Monk at 73
Looking out into the crowd and seeing nothing but vultures
See New York City
See Ohio
See Tennessee
See St. Louis
See the vultures circling high above
Foundations forever crumbling

I heard they was looking for the Blues well here I am
So what do you want to do
Here I am Redline Jones
Here I am Jane & Jim crow

Scan digital eyes pass go
Collect nothing Pay tax
See this is what it is
Ain't no map
It's one star
Sometimes you see it
Sometimes you don't
And aint nobody gon be waiting for you
Cep' all the ghosts
Coming to you to find out what happened
To sweet home
To all the diamonds,
To all the music
To all the rituals

AUTHOR BIO
Camae Ayewa (Moor Mother)

Musician, Composer & Poet, and Professor at USC Thornton School of Music

Camae is a co-founder of Black Quantum Futurism theory and practice. Black Quantum Futurism aims to uplift the intersections of experiences that are too often missing from mainstream narratives of race, gender, class, and representation. Through the theory and lens of Black Quantum Futurism, she works as a community anthropologist, uncovering hidden histories and nurturing space for building futures by sharing multigenerational stories as sonic remembrance and chronicle.

As a member of Black Quantum Futurism Collective with Rasheedah Phillips, she has been a part of several literary works, including experimental sound works, and has presented, exhibited and performed at Documenta 15 in Kassel, Germany; The Serpentine Galleries in London; Philadelphia Museum of Art; Chicago Architecture Biennial, ICA London, Le Gaite Lyrique, Guggenheim, Baltic Biennale,Pearlman Gallery, The Metropolitan Museum of Art in New York, Art Institute in Chicago, ICA Philadelphia, Bergan Kunsthall, Hirshhorn Gallery, and The Kitchen NYC.

She is a Pew Fellow, Knight Foundation Art and Technology fellow, A Blade of Grass Fellow, Leeway Transformation Award, Foundations for Contemporary Arts Fellow, Moog Sound Lab Resident,Wysing Arts Resident. She has had her work exhibited at Brooklyn Museum of Art, The Kitchen, Western Front, Serpentine Gallery, Manifesta 13, Arts at CERN, Chicago Architecture Biennial.

American Equations in Black Classical Music by Camae Ayewa
First North American Edition, 2024
Copyright © 2024 by Camae Ayewa
All rights reserved.

Identifiers: 978-1-955125-42-0

Subject: BISAC: Poetry / American / African American & Black
Cover Design: Matt Dorffman
Interior Design: Abe Ogden

Printed in Europe by Oddi.

ISBN: 978-1-955125-42-0

Hat & Beard Editions books are published by:

Hat & Beard, LLC
713 N. La Fayette Park Place
Los Angeles, CA 90026

www.hatandbeard.com
IG: @hatandbeardpress

H&
B

H
&
B

H&
B

HAT & BEARD PRESS

H
&B

H&B

H
&B